Teaching About Cultural Awareness

George Otero

with

Gary Smith

CENTER FOR TEACHING
INTERNATIONAL
R E L A T I O N S

For further information about the other CTIR publications and programs, please call 303-871-3106, or visit our web site at **www.du.edu/ctir**.

CTIR Publications

BRINGING THE WORLD TO YOUR CLASSROOM

CENTER FOR TEACHING
INTERNATIONAL
R E L A T I O N S

University of Denver
Graduate School of International Studies

For over 35 years, the Center for Teaching International Relations (CTIR) has published high quality materials on international studies for use in K–12 classrooms. As an integral part of the University of Denver Graduate School of International Studies, CTIR is dedicated to improving public understanding of international affairs.

CTIR materials are designed to provide a balanced presentation of information with the goal of fostering critical thinking about international issues. Our age-appropriate lesson plans are written in conjunction with award-winning classroom teachers and are strategically presented in a modular format from which teachers can choose the most relevant lessons for their specific classrooms. Each lesson is:

- Activity oriented
- Based on national education content standards
- Designed to help students prepare for standardized testing
- Written to incorporate language arts and logical thinking skills

CTIR materials fit easily into a classroom curriculum because they are based on core subject matters such as economics, history, civics, geography, and science. By addressing these subjects in an international context, students gain both an understanding of contemporary international events as well as the foundations upon which they are based. CTIR materials provide students with tools to successfully navigate an increasingly global environment.

CENTER FOR TEACHING
INTERNATIONAL
R E L A T I O N S

We want to hear from you!

Your comments on this publication will help us develop
materials that suit your needs.

Visit our web site to:

- **Complete our survey**
- **Download *free* materials**
- **Join our mailing list**

www.du.edu/ctir

800-967-2847

Internet Resources

By purchasing this book you now have access to a new service provided by CTIR. The Lesson Hand-Outs and Activities included in this book are now available in an easy to download format on our website. Instead of making copies from the book, we invite you to download all of the handouts at once.

It's quick and easy to do. Just go to **www.du.edu/ctir**, click on Publications, and select Teacher Resources. After filling in your name you will be directed to a list of all CTIR books from which you may choose from any of the titles that you have purchased from us. From here you will need a password to open the file.

The password for *Teaching Cultural Awareness* is: **Diversity**

(Note: The Passwords are case sensitive)

TABLE OF CONTENTS

INTRODUCTION   1
  Goals   2
  Rationale   2
  Major Concepts Used   3
  The Sections   3
  Teaching Strategies   4
  When and Where to Use the Activities   4

SECTION ONE: PERCEPTION   5
  Introduction   7
  Behind Our Eyes   9
  The Woman   17
  Rumor Clinic   22
  You Kids Are All Alike   24
  Sorting Out Terms   29
  Faces   31
  Images of the Chinese and Japanese through Gallup Polls   48
  My Images   50
  Draw Me a Picture   53
  "Declaration of Independence--That "Commie Junk'"
    and "Perspective   56

SECTION TWO: CULTURE AND ME   59
  Introduction   61
  What Is Culture?   62
  My Attitude Toward Diverse Ethnic Groups   64
  Family Influences on Attitudes Toward Ethnic Groups 65
  Ethnicity In My Life   67
  Labels   72
  Groups and Social Distance   75
  Which Differences Matter?   80
  Family Search and Research   83
  "Body Ritual Among the Nacirema"   85
  Cronies, Dandis, and Others   90

SECTION THREE: CULTURAL CONFLICT, DISCRIMINATION, AND
INSTITUTIONAL RACISM   97
  Introduction   99
  The Prejudiced Personality   100
  A Bunch of Groups   102
  Paradoxes of Prejudice   104
  Put Yourself In My Shoes   108
  The Will   110
  Alabama Literacy Test   113
  An Ethnic TV Guide   116
  Racism: Institutional Dimensions   119
  Planning Multicultural Communities   124
  Culture and the School, A Checklist   128

The major goal of teaching cultural awareness is to raise students' consciousness about cultural differences: to help them become aware of the diversity of ideas and practices found in human societies, of how these ideas and practices compare, and of recognizing their own cultural orientation and perspective. In this program we look at culture broadly, encouraging students to become more conscious of the role culture plays in their lives and in global society.

Acquiring such perspective is a difficult task to accomplish. It is one thing to have information about other cultures; it is another to deal with the issues generated from the human capacity for creating different cultures--with the resulting profound differences in outlook and practice manifested within society. Human differences are widely known at the level of myth and stereotype, but they are not deeply and truly known, in spite of the popular exhortation to "understand others."* This program encourages students to dig deeper into the power of culture in our lives. Such acceptance seems to be resisted by powerful forces within humans. Differences appear to matter the most when we feel uncomfortable with them. There is a disturbing feeling that comes when our well-established behavior and thinking patterns are interrupted by contact with contrasting values and practices. Attainment of cultural awareness and empathy requires experiences and strategies that counter many of these tendencies. Another major purpose of this volume is to provide suggestions for teaching some of the experiences and strategies that counter many of these forces of resistance.

Culture just may be the most powerful force in the contempory world. Becoming more aware of culture and its influences in our lives becomes a basic skill in today's world.

Becoming culturally aware requires an understanding of the processes of human perception and how multiple perspectives and diverse cultural orientations are basic to the fabric of life among humans. Cultural awareness is also enhanced by looking closely at our own personal acculturation experiences. This means taking time to explore our own ethnic heritage, learning the specific manifestations of cultural universals. And finally, cultural awareness can be piqued by studying the conflicts that culture processes in a global society where contact and interaction between different peoples is daily fare. Issues like ageism, racism, sexism, and classism all share certain basic cultural dynamics that if understood hold promise for better opportunity for resolution, true tolerance and more humble, compassionate coping.

---

*An Attainable Global Perspective by Robert G. Hanvey. NY: American Forum, 1975

©CTIR
University of Denver

Goals

The general goals of this volume will be to:

1. Stimulate positive attitudes in students about the role of cultural differences in their lives.

2. Recognize the functions of self and culture--values, personal feelings, attitudes, beliefs--in fostering and inhibiting cultural interaction and awareness.

3. Develop an awareness of how change can occur within students and institutions so that everyone can fully realize their creative potential.

4. Expose students to methods and strategies for learning about cultural differences.

Rationale

Four ideas about cultural awareness underlie these activities and strategies:

1. <u>Largely because of culture, humans have differing values and perceptions of the world.</u> This means there is a need to perceive and act differently toward them. To assume that there is one proper way to behave toward all human beings is both naive and unworkable. When one travels in a foreign country, for example, s/he soon learns that adjustments in thinking and behaving must be made because of the different cultural context. Ties to the nation-state notwithstanding, it is reasonable to apply this same principle to cultural and minority groups within our own society.

2. <u>Humans in many ways are captives of their culture.</u> Each of us operates within the confines of training, socialization, and tradition. In large measure, we do so to survive. But we need to become aware that we act as if our behavior should be logical to others because our frame of reference is hidden below the conscious level. We are like icebergs. The bulk of the iceberg is that part of perspective which is ordinarily unexamined and unquestioned. Awareness of our own perspective involves stepping over the consciousness threshold to examine behaviors and assumptions that are ordinarily set in motion when we are confronted with human differences. Hence, cultural awareness is as much about "us" and "me" as it is about "them." The authors feel you will learn more about yourself than you will learn about the culture you are studying.

3. <u>There are some potentially destructive common ways humans respond to cultural and ethnic differences.</u> These include stereotyping, ethnocentrism, prejudice, and discrimination. As part of cultural awareness, students need to know how these mechanisms work. The materials provide the opportunity for examination of a number of cultural and ethnic groups. It is the process of perception and communication that seems paramount in cultural awareness. These same processes can be applied to a study of <u>any cultural group</u>. Moreover, students can look at these mechanisms more objectively if

the groups examined are not those with whom they are experiencing conflict in the school.

4. There is great diversity within cultural groups. This means that we cannot simply develop a codebook for any culture's behavior and apply it to all members of the group. No codebook for behavior can or should be developed. Limiting our education about cultural groups to how "they" do things as opposed to how "we" do things denies individual and subgroup identity within a larger cultural group. Moreover, we tend to substitute one set of stereotypes for another. In fact, there are more differences within a culture, than there are between any two cultural groups.

Major   Concepts

PERCEPTION: In the context of this unit, perception refers to the process by which we receive and process information and images about "other" groups of people. Specifically, the materials focus on visual perception, stereotyping, and using diverse data to change stereotyped images.

CULTURE: A very nebulous term, the concept refers to a distinct set of values, norms, beliefs, and standards by which groups of people are viewed as different from each other. Culture also implies shared beliefs and values among members of the group.

DISCRIMINATION: It is the "acting out" of prejudice. Discrimination refers to behavior, whereas prejudice and ethnocentrism refer to discriminatory attitudes.

CULTURAL CONFLICT: Ethnic differences, whether real or perceived, are at the root of a large portion of human conflict. The conflict can be between groups of people, or within and between countries. When we begin to understand how we are culturally different, we may begin to understand the necessity for finding approaches to manage or avoid conflict while maintaining our own identities.

INSTITUTIONAL RACISM: It includes practices and systemic behavior, whether intentional or simply a result of tradition, which discriminate against a particular racial or ethnic group. What is paramount is that the discrimination is systemic; it is often sanctioned in institutional practice.

The   Sections

This book consists of three interrelated sections about cultural awareness. Each section is composed of lessons which can be used or left out of the section or unit you're teaching, depending on the students' needs and their levels of cultural awareness. Descriptions of the sections follow.

Section One: PERCEPTION--focuses on the processes humans use to view differences. Includes activities on stereotyping and the role of introducing diverse data to deal with the dysfunctional aspects of stereotypic images.

Section Two: CULTURE AND ME--concentrates on developing the awareness that we are all members and captives of culture, and on how we operate verbally and nonverbally to act out cultural roles. Includes a set of experiences which place students in different cultural contexts to increase consciousness about their own perspectives. A number of activities also help young people explore their own cultural or ethnic heritage.

Section Three: CULTURAL CONFLICT, DISCRIMINATION, AND INSTITUTIONAL RACISM--offers readings and a simulation game which explore the structural and systemic nature of institutional racism. The goal is awareness, of the many conflicts in global society today that cannot be understood without an awareness of how culture affects us all, the ability of participants to recognize where and when institutional racism exists, and how it contributes to unhealthy conflict.

Teaching Strategies

These activities depart from the standard lecture-read teaching approaches found in most curriculum materials. Whenever possible, students are presented with opportunities to role-play and experience their own levels of cultural awareness. Moreover, the variety of strategies employed departs from the "read and recite" format of many conventional curriculum materials.

Many activities employ discussion as their primary teaching strategy. However, instead of simply giving students a topic or concept to discuss, the lessons provide an activity or starter exercise to spur interest in the topic or issue. Discussion can then proceed with more enthusiasm. Other teaching strategies used are roleplaying, gaming, and use of community resources.

When and Where to Use the Activities

These activities are designed to be used with upper elementary, junior, and senior high school students. They are supplementary materials and are not intended to provide a sequential unit of study. Each activity is labeled with an appropriate grade level. However, with a little adaptation most activities can be used with younger students than indicated.

In the school curriculum these materials are appropriate for use in just about any course of study related to culture and ethnicity. Specifically, they can be used in world history, world cultures, minority history and cultures, sociology, anthropology, psychology, and general social studies in elementary, junior, and senior high grades.

SECTION ONE

PERCEPTION

Reality happens to be, like a landscape
possessed of an infinite number of perspectives,
all equally veracious and authentic. The sole
false perspective is that which claims to be
the only one there is.

Jose Ortega y Gasset

Cultural awareness is sensitivity to cultural differences. It involves more than taking on new information about a particular cultural group or groups. Developing sensitivity to differences means examining our perceptions and trying on new behaviors to fit different cultural contexts. This section represents an initial step in reaching the awareness goal. It includes activities and readings that help us find out what stereotypes and perceptions we hold and encourages us to consider the intentions that form those views.

Stereotypes affect what we think and believe about others as well as how we behave towards them. These images allow us to treat people in certain groups differently than we would if our thinking were less rigid, more tentative. Stereotyping often serves as a substitute for thinking. We often tend to stereotype to avoid contact with those people we perceive as being "fundamentally" different from us. "You know how gypsies are; you wouldn't want to associate with one, would you?" Such a statement illustrates how stereotyping operates. According to the stereotype, it would be senseless to interact with a gypsy because "We all know what they're like anyway." Things are set. We want to unsettle the mind of the student and open them to multiple perspectives.

A note of caution, there is a critical difference between categorizing and stereotyping. Because of the amount of information we have to assimilate, categorizing is necessary. It is a way to reduce and simplify an otherwise impossibly complex world. Stereotypes, as we use them in this program, go beyond the functionality of thinking in categories. They are beliefs about people in categories that lessen the chances of interaction and diminish the potential for recognizing and accepting differences. If we conclude, for example, that because someone has red hair he is quick-tempered, then we are evaluating him on the basis of a stereotype.

Stereotype formation seems to be influenced in two basic ways: (1) the type of information we receive about a group, and (2) our predisposition and preconditioning (attitudes) about the group. ("The Woman" activity brings out the role of preconditioning.) It would be possible for us to break through many of the more dysfunctional aspects of stereotyping if "new" information were introduced to us about the group that is stereotyped.

It is only a possibility that stereotypic thinking will change, however. Whenever humans hold rigid beliefs about others and there seem to be payoffs in holding these beliefs, there is a strong tendency to simply disregard "new" diverse information about a group. Such an investment in one's beliefs leads to selectively perceiving information that reinforces the beliefs. ("Rumor Clinic" demonstrates to students how selective perception works.) Much of this process occurs at an unconscious level. At a minimum, it would be beneficial to examine how this process operates within each of us.

7   ©CTIR
                                   University of Denver

Finally, our stereotypes say far more about us than they do about those people we are stereotyping. When we state a judgment or opinion, it is ours. It does not describe reality--it is only our rather biased assessment of reality. "People on welfare are lazy" says much more about persons holding that view than it does about people on welfare. Accordingly, <u>this section can provide a good means for examining what we believe and why we believe it</u>.

Introduction

This first activity introduces the concept of perception with a set of drawings. The idea it presents is this. Our brains process information in ways that conflict with what we have learned to see. There are physical processes that dominate our reception of data from the external world. How we interpret what we see is explained in this Chinese proverb, "We see what is behind our eyes."

Objectives

Students will be able to:

- Describe how beliefs they have learned affect the way figures are perceived.
- Generate at least one hypothesis concerning the implication of misperceiving other people.

Grade Level

4-12

Time

One class period

Materials

Handout #1, "Ten Figures"
Chalkboard and chalk

Procedures

1. Write the proverb on the chalkboard: "We see what is behind our eyes."

2. Ask students to explain what they think the proverb means. Don't spend too much time on this. There will be opportunity in the next step for further discussion.

3. Distribute Handout #1 to students. Explain that figures 1 through 10 on the handout illustrate one interpretation of the proverb. Following is a guide for taking participants through the drawings on the handout.

Fig. 1:   Which one of the two horizontal lines is longer?

Answer: Both lines are the same length. What causes us to be misled is not clearly understood. Psychologists tell us that we are influenced by the other lines in the drawing (context) which lead us to make wrong guesses about what we perceive. Even though we know the answer, our eyes tell us differently.

Fig. 2:   Are the horizontal lines straight?

Answer: Yes, even though they appear to be bent. The illusion is caused, in part, by our interpretation of the lines in context with the other lines.

Fig. 3:   Are the horizontal lines straight?

Answer: Yes. (Same reason as given for Figure 2.)

9   ©CTIR
University of Denver

Fig. 4: Does the square have straight sides or are they bowed inward?

Answer: The square has straight sides, even though we perceive them as being bowed.

Fig. 5: Is the cube facing left or right?

Answer: Possibly, either way. Our perceptions keep changing!

Fig. 6: Which way through the coils--left or right?

Answer: Possibly, either way. Our perceptions keep changing.

Fig. 7: Do you see a flight of stairs or an overhanging cornice?

Answer: Possibly, either.

Fig. 8: Do you perceive movement in this drawing?

Answer: Most people do because of the involuntary movement of the eye.

Fig. 9: Is this a "possible figure" or an "impossible" one? Follow the stairs around and try to determine whether they're going up or down.

Fig. 10: Is this a "possible figure" or an "impossible" one? Try to imagine what the triangle would look like in a three-dimensional plane.

4. Pick out a few of the drawings and see if you can deduce a central theme about them. (Perhaps "Seeing is not believing.")

• How do you explain why you might be fooled by some of the figures, if you had not seen them before or "gotten the point" of the activity?

• Can you suggest what the Chinese proverb means after having looked at the drawings? (One possible interpretation is that the source of illusions and misperceptions must be sought in the mind, not in the brain.)

5. Explain the statement, "Context or background affects the way we perceive things."

6. Suggest some problems that might arise when you misperceive other people.

Follow-up

Ask students to create hypotheses about how visual perception might affect cultural understanding. List these hypotheses on the chalkboard or butcher paper.

Some hypotheses which might be generated are:

- What we perceive can be misleading;

- Perceptions depend on context, particularly cultural context;

- Different people have different perceptions of the same stimulus; and

- All perceptions may be equally valid.

TEN FIGURES

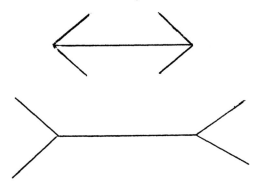

Figure 1

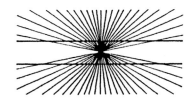

Figure 2

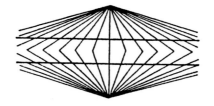

Figure 3

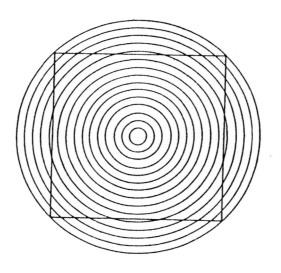

Figure 4

13

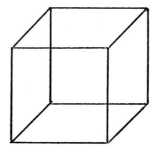

Figure 5

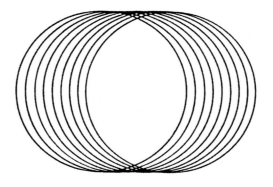

Figure 6

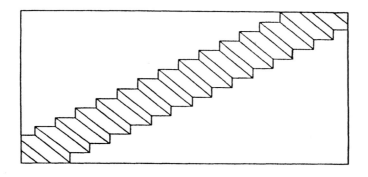

Figure 7

Figure 8

15

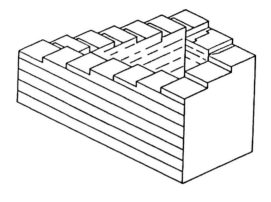

Figure 9

Figure 10

16

Introduction

"Behind Our Eyes" introduces the idea that what we perceive can be misleading. This activity, however, demonstrates the importance of programming or preconditioning when perceiving certain things. To perform this activity, you must be able to make and show transparencies.

Objective

Students will be able to:

- Become aware of how preconditioning and socialization affects cultural awareness.

Grade Level

4-12

Time

One class period or less

Materials

Handout #2, "Perception"
Make transparencies of the three drawings
Overhead projector and screen

Procedure

1. Ask half of the class to stand and face away from the screen. Tell the group seated that you are about to show them a drawing on the screen which they should study silently for about five seconds. Show transparency A to seated group for no longer than five seconds, then turn off projector. Ask group that was standing to turn around and be seated.

2. Ask group that was seated in step 1 to stand up and face away from the screen. Tell group seated that you are about to show them a drawing on the screen which they should study for about five seconds. Show transparency B to seated group for no longer than five seconds, then turn off projector. Ask group that was standing to turn around and be seated.

3. Show entire group transparency C.

4. Discuss with the class the following:

- How many people see an old woman? How many see a young woman? Both? Usually, most people in the first group see the young woman and most people in the second group see the old woman because they were <u>preconditioned, programmed,</u> or <u>socialized</u> to do so.

5. Ask people in each group to explain to persons in the other group where the outline of "their" woman is. Pass out copies of the first two figures for this purpose or show each group the other group's transparency.

- What would it mean to say some of you were <u>programmed</u> or <u>socialized</u> to see one woman or the other?

©CTIR
University of Denver

6. Ask students to state what implications this programming has for us in forming images of peoples in other national, cultural, or ethnic groups. List what the students state on the chalkboard.

For example:

• Control of what we see is important--it is also important to look at what "locks" us into seeing one thing to the exclusion of other things;

• All cultural perceptions are preconditioned by past experiences;

• People perceive the same cultures in different ways based on their preconditioning or past experiences;

• Cultural preconditioning is unconscious.

7. A key to cultural awareness is knowing that you see what your experience tells you to see. Who is better prepared for the world today? Those who see the old woman, the young woman, or both?

Mention that cultural awareness has many layers. The key to seeing the old woman and the young woman is to look beyond whether you see a figure. You must notice where your focus is on the page. That awareness will free the student to see both women.

PERCEPTION

A

20

C

21

Introduction

As a result of "The Woman," students should begin to see how much programming or preconditioning can influence what we see. The much-used technique in this activity is based upon experiments conducted by Allport and Postman in the United States in the 1940s and further developed by the Anti-Defamation League of B'nai B'rith.

Objectives

Students will be able to:

• Become aware of negative aspects of rumors.
• Understand how powerful our experience is in determining how we interpret what is going on in the world around us.

Grade Level

4-12

Time

One class period

Materials

A picture of your choosing taken from a current magazine

Procedure

1. Choose six students to be reporters. Choose one person to be door keeper. Send the six reporters out of the room, and explain to the group that they will now have a chance to see what happens to a story as it is told and retold. Introduce the clinic to the rest of the group, saying something as follows:

> **This is a demonstration to show you how a rumor grows as it travels. Six volunteers have been picked to act as reporters. A picture will be shown to you to study. We will call in the first reporter, who will be the only one of the six to see the picture with you. He will study it, and then tell the next reporter as much as he can remember from the picture. Then, reporter number 2 (any one of the remaining five) will repeat the story to reporter number 3, and so on, until each reporter has had a chance to tell the story. As the report is passed on from person to person, we will watch to see what changes take place in the story as it is passed along. After the reporters have finished, we will begin a discussion on why the changes in the story were made.**

2. Show the group the picture. About sixty seconds of exposure to the picture will do. Caution the rest of the class not to laugh, comment, or coach the reporters in any way during the demonstration. Also, be sure that the reporters talk loudly enough for the entire group to hear.

3. Ask the door keeper to bring in reporter #1. Let him look at the picture for about thirty seconds. Then ask him to turn the picture face down on a table.

4. Call in reporter #2, but don't let him see the picture. Ask reporter #1 to describe the scene in the picture.

5. Bring in reporter #3. Ask reporter #2 to repeat the story he has just heard from reporter #1.

6. Continue until each reporter has heard and retold the story. Let reporter #6 tell the whole group his version of the story told him by reporter #5.

7. Ask the students:

• What elements in the picture were <u>omitted</u> as the story was told and retold? Why?

• What was <u>added</u> to the story as it was passed along? Why?

• How is selectivity connected with prejudice, stereotyping, and cultural awareness?

• What are implications of the activity for what we hear and read?

Follow-up

Have students state what implications selectivity of perception has for cultural awareness. List their responses on the chalkboard. Possible implications would be:

• We hear and see what we wish to;

• Selectivity is connected with our preconditioning;

• We often select items about others based on ethnic and cultural perceptions; and

• Most perception selection is done unconsciously.

Introduction   This is an introductory exercise on stereotyping. It illustrates the point that we all have stereotypes and that they can be dysfunctional.

Objectives   Students will be able to:

- Become familiar with the term stereotype.
- Better understand how stereotypes limit our thinking.

Grade   Level   6-12

Time   One class period

Materials   Handout #3, "You Kids Are All Alike"

Procedure   1. Distribute Handout #3 and ask students to read and fill out appropriate parts of the reading.

2. Hold a class discussion.

- According to what you know and read in the readings, what is a stereotype? (An image of a group of people that labels every member of that group with the same characteristics.)

- Do all people, except infants, have stereotypes? (The question is a bit rhetorical, but necessary to ask. The answer is "Yes," as far as we know.)

- List all the circumstances you can think of when stereotyping can be harmful. Are they harmful to the group or individual being stereotyped? To you?

©CTIR
University of Denver

YOU KIDS ARE ALL ALIKE

Let's suppose it's the week before Christmas and you're given the task of buying a present for each of the following people:

1. Harry Skinner, a cab driver
2. Marsha Truelove, a food bank volunteer
3. Freddy Faster, a sixth-grade "A" student
4. Abigail Watson, a senior citizen

Which of the following gifts would you choose for each?

a desk dictionary   _____

a rocking chair   _____

two tickets to the opera   _____

a pair of skis   _____

a leather jacket   _____

a makeup kit   _____

a popular record album   _____

a first-aid kit   _____

Did you choose:

• The leather jacket for Harry because "it's the kind of clothing a cab driver wears";

• The first-aid kit for Marsha since "it may come in handy the next time she helps out in an emergency";

• The desk dictionary for Freddy who "can always use a dictionary to help him with his studies";

• The rocker for Abigail who "probably doesn't get around too much and who spends most of the time staring out the window."

No doubt these are the "usual" choices. But the people on our list happen to be "unusual." They don't fit into such neat categories.

• Harry is a voice student who drives a cab in his spare time. He has nothing against leather jackets, but he'd prefer the opera tickets. He hopes to become an opera singer one of these days.

• At 16, Marsha listens to her favorite popular music while doing volunteer work at the food bank every afternoon. She doesn't need a first-aid kit to sort groceries.

- Freddy is working on a clown routine for the school Talent Show right now. A makeup kit would help his act a lot more than a dictionary would.

- Born in Vermont, Abigail still enjoys skiing down a powdery slope on a brisk winter's day. She would put those new skis to good use, and has no need of a rocking chair just yet.

Did the labels on these people mislead you into making the "usual" choices? Then you read too much into them. To know a person well you need a great deal of information, more than you'll find on a label. With nothing but a word or two to go on, your mind produced a stereotyped picture rather than a real one.

In printing, a "stereotype" is a metal plate which reproduces the same picture over and over. In thinking, a stereotype is a mental picture. It has all people in a particular group looking and acting the same way. Stereotypes can cloud our judgment because they ignore the fact that no two human beings are identical. People just aren't.

Take the cab driver, for example. In your mind did you picture him as a middle-aged, rugged, boisterous, gabby family man? This is one stereotype of a "cabbie"--the one you usually meet on TV or in movies. But real cab drivers can be young or old, sensitive, educated, softspoken, shy, unmarried, and either male or female. Yet, when we think in stereotypes, we tend to ignore this.

Here are some other examples of stereotypes. Do you recognize them?

1. She wears her hair tied in a bun.
    She wears horn-rimmed glasses.
    She's a spinster.
    She's always saying "sh" to people.
    She spends her days surrounded by books.

    She is a _____

2. He's fast talking and fast moving.
    His secretary adores and worships him.
    He's fearless and can take a beating as well as give one.
    He usually outwits the police.
    His clients often include beautiful women.

    He is a _____

3. She's a big, meddlesome lady with a loud voice.
    She pays surprise visits to her children.
    She's fond of saying, "my poor baby."
    She has been known to wreck some marriages.
    She likes to spoil the children.

    She is a _____

How true-to-life are these stereotypes? Usually, a stereotype has some truth to it. There probably are some librarians who wear their hair in a bun, private eyes who are chased by beautiful women, and mothers-in-law who are pests. But there are many more who do not fit these descriptions. The danger in the stereotype is that it distorts our understanding of people by ignoring their differences.

Some adults have a way of stereotyping young people. Perhaps you have heard their argument. It goes something like this:

> **You kids are all alike. You show no respect for your elders, you have poor manners, and your speech is as sloppy as your dress. You don't realize how good you have it. Now in my day. . . ."**

The harm here is that the person who believes in this stereotype may act on this belief. In the case just mentioned, you, as a young person, would be the victim. Maybe you've already had the experience. Have you ever met a merchant who doesn't trust kids in his store? A bus driver who hates all kids who go to that school on the hill? A teacher who is suspicious of a boy with long hair?

Stereotypes are often used by the mass media--by TV, advertising, the movies, magazines, comics, etc. Sometimes these stereotypes are amusing and entertaining. The henpecked husband, the absent-minded professor, the preppy student, all make us laugh because they are such exaggerations of the real thing.

The mass media rely on the fact that all of us have certain stereotypes in our heads. For example, the column at the left lists a number of different types of people. Can you match the person to the quality in the right-hand column with which he or she is usually associated?

1. BLONDES	a. are disrespectful of adults
2. FAT PEOPLE	b. aren't scholars
3. REDHEADS	c. make false promises
4. ATHLETES	d. have more fun
5. PROFESSORS	e. are glamorous
6. POLITICIANS	f. are hot-tempered
7. TEENAGERS	g. are always happy
8. ACTRESSES	h. are absent-minded

Stereotypes distort the truth. They suggest that all people in a particular group behave in the same way. They also suggest that only these people behave that way. Neither is true.

When people begin to stereotype others on the basis of their race, religion, or nationality, the result is prejudice. Archie Bunker, the "loveable" bigot of TV's "All In The Family" was guilty of this. Archie, like most bigots, saw only what he wanted to see. Instead of judging people on their merits and abilities, he identified them with a race or religion or nationality and then either praised or blasted them.

It is important to remember that no one group in our society has a monopoly on brawling, laziness, ignorance, foreign accents, drinking, crime, greed, pushiness, etc. Nor does any one group have a monopoly on beauty, brains, glamor, strength, humor, talent, etc. Every group has its share of all of these human qualities.

To be sure, a certain amount of stereotyping is bound to occur. We all do it--usually without thinking about it. But it's a good idea to remember that no two people in the world are identical. Thus, no label can be pasted on an individual or group that accurately describes that person or group. After all, labels belong on products, not people.

28

Introduction   In this activity students become more aware of their own tendency to stereotype.

Objective   Students will be able to:

- Become familiar with the meaning of stereotyping, prejudice, dislike, and misconception.

Grade Level   9-12

Time   One class period

Materials   Handout #4, "Statements"

Procedure   1. Distribute Handout #4 to students and have them read the statements.

2. Then ask:

- Which of the statements on the handout illustrate a <u>stereotype</u>? Which of them show <u>prejudice</u>? Which show a <u>dislike</u> based on a reason--or a difference in taste? <u>Which show a misconception</u>?

- How do your responses compare with others in the group?

- How would you define each of the four terms?

- In what ways are these terms interrelated? For what reasons and under what circumstances should we recognize their different meanings?

3. Ask students to define each of the terms.

<u>Stereotype</u> (Suggested answer: A generalized mental picture held about members of a certain group.)

<u>Prejudice</u> (Suggested answer: Preconceived judgment or opinion of someone else without sufficient data. Often applied to attitudes about ethnic or racial groups because of preconceived negative notions about those groups.)

<u>Dislike</u> (Suggested answer: Usually based on personal preference. One who dislikes someone or something else <u>may</u> have a great deal of information before forming an opinion.)

<u>Misconception</u> (Suggested answer: Implies misinformation or mistaken information.)

STATEMENTS

1. "I won't eat peaches; I don't like the way they smell."

2. "Peaches cause cancer. I knew a man who ate a lot of peaches. He died of cancer. Our doctor says peaches are good for you. But I still say they cause cancer."

3. "I wouldn't let my daughter date a boy who rides a motorcycle. I know what they're like!"

4. "I thought all boys with earrings were gay 'til I met Fred. Now I know how wrong I was."

5. "I have no use for Ann. She is a braggart and a show-off. I can't stand to be around her."

6. "Wallonians are dishonest and lazy. I've seen some of them, and I know what I'm talking about."

7. "I thought people on welfare were lazy until I met Jerry's family. Then I got a different idea about the whole thing."

Introduction

This activity will help break down the stereotypes that "all Chinese look alike" and have stereotypic facial characteristics. All of the drawings included in the activity were done by Chinese in 1973 in the People's Republic of China.

Objective

Students will be able to:

• Become aware of the effects of stereotyping physical appearances.

Grade Level

1-12

Time

One class period

Materials

Handout #5, "Face Drawings"

Procedure

1. Distribute the drawings one at a time. Ask students to write down the name of a country or place in the world they think the person in the drawing is from. Provide globes or world maps.

2. Spend a few minutes listing on the chalkboard all the different places students have indicated. Ask their reasons for making the choices they did. (Explore their stereotypes.)

3. Inform students that all of the drawings are of Chinese people and that they were drawn by people in the People's Republic of China during 1973.

4. Ask:

• How did this activity affect your images of the Chinese? (Hopefully, it will have helped to break down the stereotype many people hold that "all Chinese look alike.")

• How do people learn stereotypes such as "All Chinese look alike"?

• What could we do to challenge views that are simplistic? (We can provide diverse views as this activity does.)

• Do this activity for other cultural or ethnic groups. Use magazines for pictures.

---

*Based on an exercise suggested by H. Thomas Collins, Elliott School of International Affairs, George Washington University.

FACE DRAWINGS

33

35

37

38

40

41

42

43

45

46

47

Introduction

Gallup polls taken at different time periods can reveal a great deal about the changeability of people's perceptions regarding other racial groups. We can hypothesize about why the changes in perception occurred and about why certain characteristics prevail.

Objective

Students will be able to:

• Analyze data in an international historical context.

Grade Level

6-12

Time

One class period

Materials

Handout #6, "Images of the Chinese and Japanese"

Procedure

1. Pass out copies of Handout #6 and have students read the material.

2. Ask students to make hypotheses about why the changes in perceptions might have occurred in the different time periods. Ask them to list at least three hypotheses.

3. Compile a list of hypotheses on the chalkboard from the list made in step #2 above.

4. Ask students the following questions:

• How would you go about checking your hypotheses for correctness about changing images of the Chinese and Japanese? (Old periodicals, magazines, newspapers, etc., to check out the "climate of opinion" of the times; current survey of attitudes using the same adjectives in the participants' community, etc.)

• Which adjectives on the handout seem to apply to both the Japanese and Chinese? (Tendency to lump "Orientals" together in peoples' minds.)

• What are the three most commonly used adjectives for each group according to the handout? Where do you suppose these images came from?

• Ask students to brainstorm ways to check out their hypotheses made in steps 2 and 3 above. Then ask them to locate data to verify their hypotheses.

Follow-up

Conduct a survey using the adjectives on the sheet for your community for the current year. What do you find to be your community's current images about Japanese?

IMAGES OF THE CHINESE AND JAPANESE*

The following sets of percentages relating to the Chinese and the Japanese (George Gallup Polls) are taken from a sampling made in 1942, just after Pearl Harbor when the Chinese had become the United States' "heroic allies" and the Japanese attacking foes; and again in 1966, when the Chinese had long since become the foe and Japan the ally; and in March 1972, just after United States President Richard M. Nixon's trip to Beijing. The selection of adjectives is as follows:

CHINESE

	1942	1966	1972
	Percentages		
Hardworking	69	37	74
Honest	52	-	20
Brave	48	7	17
Religious	33	14	18
Intelligent	24	14	32
Practical	23	8	27
Ignorant	22	24	10
Artistic	21	13	26
Progressive	14	7	28
Sly	8	20	19
Treacherous	4	19	12
Warlike	4	23	13
Cruel	3	13	9

JAPANESE

	1942	1966
	Percentages	
Treacherous	73	12
Sly	63	19
Cruel	56	9
Warlike	46	11
Hardworking	39	44
Intelligent	25	35
Brave	24	17
Religious	20	18
Progressive	19	31
Artistic	19	31
Ignorant	16	4
Practical	9	17
Honest	2	9

*Harold R. Isaacs, IMAGES OF ASIA: AMERICAN VIEWS OF CHINA AND INDIA (New York: Harper and Row, 1972), pp. xviii-xix. Copyright 1958 by Massachusetts Institute of Technology. Reprinted by permission of publisher and author.

Introduction   This activity documents student images of older persons, and asks the students to consider the experiences they have had which generate these images.

Objective   Students will be able to:

- Analyze diverse information about a culture, ethnic group, or segment of society.

Grade Level   6-12

Time   One class period

Materials   Handout #7, "Instructions for My Images"
Handout #8, "My Images"

Procedures   1. Distribute Handout #7 and have students review the instructions.

2. Distribute Handout #8 and have students complete the survey.

3. Gather up the surveys and tabulate, if desired, on the chalkboard.

4. Discuss the results with them, bringing out where they obtained their impressions and their feelings.

- Did you find it difficult to do the survey? If so, why?

- Are there some stereotypic views that most students have of older persons?

- How could you test these images? How could you determine the validity of these images?

- What role does the media play in determining our images of older persons?

©CTIR
University of Denver

INSTRUCTION FOR "MY IMAGES"

You are asked to participate in a survey to find out how you view older persons. Since this kind of survey might be new to you, a few examples will help you complete it.

The example here has no relationship to older persons. It is merely used to show you the mechanics of answering the survey.

Suppose you were given the following statement and set of words:

I THINK THE WORLD WE LIVE IN TODAY IS . . .

STABLE   1   2   3   4   5   6   7   UNSTABLE

You would think for a moment about how you view world stability. If you think the world is extremely unstable, you would probably circle the 7 to indicate your view. If you think the world is very unstable, or simply unstable, you might circle the 5 or 6; somewhat stable, circle the 3 of 4; very stable, circle the 2; extremely stable, circle the 1.

There is no attempt to trick you with the questions. Please answer all questions honestly and to the best of your ability. DO NOT PUT YOUR NAME ON THE SURVEY UNDER ANY CIRCUMSTANCES.

NOTE: YOUR TEACHER MAY WANT TO TABULATE THE RESULTS OF THE SURVEY AND DISCUSS GROUP RESPONSE TO THE ITEMS.

MY IMAGES

Please CIRCLE the number on the word scale that best expresses your views for each set of words.

"WHEN I THINK OF OLDER PERSONS, I THINK OF PEOPLE WHO ARE. . ."

KIND	1 2 3 4 5 6 7	CRUEL
HEALTHY	1 2 3 4 5 6 7	UNHEALTHY
DISHONEST	1 2 3 4 5 6 7	HONEST
HAPPY	1 2 3 4 5 6 7	SAD
QUIET	1 2 3 4 5 6 7	LOUD
HARDWORKING	1 2 3 4 5 6 7	LAZY
BRAVE	1 2 3 4 5 6 7	COWARDLY
RELIGIOUS	1 2 3 4 5 6 7	NOT RELIGIOUS
POOR	1 2 3 4 5 6 7	RICH
INTELLIGENT	1 2 3 4 5 6 7	IGNORANT
WARLIKE	1 2 3 4 5 6 7	PEACEFUL
PROGRESSIVE	1 2 3 4 5 6 7	TRADITIONAL

Introduction   This activity is an alternative way of eliciting images of Native Americans. People of all ages carry around pictures in their heads of other peoples which are positive, negative, or neutral.

Objectives   Students will be able to:

• Become aware of different ways to stereotype a culture.
• Classify stereotypes as positive, negative, or neutral.

Grade Level   7-12

Time   One to two class periods

Materials   Large sheets of paper, one for each group
Colored markers, pencils, or crayons
Handout #9, "Descriptions"
Handout #10, "Conclusions"

Procedure   1. Divide the class into groups and have each group go to a different area of the classroom. Each group is to draw a picture of a Native American.

2. After the various groups return have them tape up the pictures around the room.

3. Pass out copies of Handout #9; ask students to fill it out.

4. Pass out copies of Handout #10; instruct students to fill out the handout.

5. After completing both handouts, ask:

• Which of the images of Native Americans you listed in this activity are <u>negative</u>? Which are <u>positive</u>? Which are <u>neither</u>? Add up the negative ones and compare the number with the number of positive and neutral ones. Are there more negative images?

• How might someone with these images act toward Native Americans?

• What difference does it make that we have images like these?

   ©CTIR
University of Denver

DESCRIPTIONS

According to the group of pictures which participants have drawn, what are Native Americans like? Use short phrase descriptions in each of the categories below that apply.

Clothing _____

_____

Hair style _____

_____

Hats _____

_____

Eyes _____

_____

Mouth and teeth _____

_____

Facial expression (happy, sad, etc.) _____

_____

Other facial features (nose, ears, etc.) _____

_____

Language (if applicable) _____

_____

How they talk _____

_____

Where they live (if applicable) _____

_____

What they're doing _____

_____

What they eat (if applicable) _____

_____

How they eat (if applicable) _____

_____

Other characteristics you notice _____

_____

CONCLUSIONS

According to the pictures and the descriptions that you wrote down in handout #9, check off the characteristics listed below that are images of Native Americans which some of the participants have.

_____	Native Americans all look alike
_____	Wear feathers
_____	Have buckteeth
_____	Wear strange clothes
_____	Are red in complexion
_____	Are happy
_____	Are sad
_____	Wear war paint
_____	Ride on horses
_____	Wear moccasins
_____	Speak broken English
_____	Have strange customs
_____	Dress alike
_____	Other images? _____

55   ©CTIR

Introduction   These two readings can be used to reinforce the idea that context and situation have a lot to do with determining perspective and meaning.

Objective   Students will be able to:

- Recognize how context or situation influences how we perceive objects, people, and people's behavior.

Grade Level   9-12

Time   One class period

Materials   Handout #11, "Declaration of Independence--That 'Commie Junk'"
Handout #12, "Perspective"

Procedure   1. Distribute copies of the two readings or simply read each article aloud to the group.

2. Ask students to state how the situation or context in each of the readings is supposed to influence the perception of the people involved.

How does each reading illustrate the importance of context or the situation in determining what was perceived or understood? (In the "Declaration" reading, the fact that the document was a typed copy meant that it would not be seen as the document that was originally drafted and, therefore, would be seen out of context. It was not the document most U.S. citizens would readily recognize as a "cornerstone" of their national heritage. In "Perspective," Susie tries to establish a context in which her grades would be seen as relatively unimportant.)

Follow-up   Have students take a situation from a newspaper or magazine and rewrite that article introducing a new situation or different context which will produce a new and different "reading" or perception of the situation.

DECLARATION -- THAT 'COMMIE JUNK'*

Shoppers were approached on Miami streets by a reporter to sign a typed copy of the Declaration of Independence. They were not told what document they were reading. Only one out of fifty persons approached agreed to sign the document in approval.

Two called it "commie junk," one threatened to call the police, and another warned MIAMI HERALD reporter Colin Dangaard, "Be careful who you show that kind of antigovernment stuff to, buddy."

A questionnaire, circulated among 300 young adults attending a Youth for Christ gathering, showed that 28 percent thought an excerpt from the Declaration was written by Lenin. The youths, mostly high school seniors, were then asked to describe briefly what sort of person they thought would make such a statement. Among other things, the author of the Declaration was called:

* "A person of communism, someone against our country."

* "A person who does not have any sense of responsibility."

* "A hippie."

* "A red-neck revolutionist."

* "Someone trying to make a change in government--probably for his own selfish reasons."

Next, Dangaard typed up the Declaration in petition form, stood all day on a sidewalk and asked middle-aged passersby to read it and sign it. Only one man agreed, and he said it would cost the pollster a quarter for his signature.

Comments from those who took the trouble to read the first three paragraphs:

* "This is the work of a raver."

* "Somebody ought to tell the FBI about this sort of rubbish."

* "Meaningless."

* "I don't go for religion, Mac."

* "The boss'll have to read this before I can let you put it in the shop window. But, politically I can tell you he don't lean that way."

---

*From an Associated Press news article, July 12, 1970. Reprinted with permission.

PERSPECTIVE

Dear Mother And Dad,

Since I left for college I have been remiss in writing and I am sorry for my thoughtlessness in not having written before. I will bring up up-to-date now, but before you read on, please sit down. You are not to read any further unless you are sitting down, okay?

Well, then, I am getting along pretty well now. The skull fracture and the concussion I got when I jumped out of the window of my dormitory when it caught on fire shortly after my arrival here is pretty well healed now. I only spent two weeks in the hospital and now I can see almost normally and only get those sick headaches once a day. Fortunately, the fire in the dormitory, and my jump, were witnessed by an attendant at the gas station near the dorm, and he was the one who called the Fire Department and the ambulance. He also visited me in the hospital and since I had nowhere to live because of the burnt-out dormitory, he was kind enough to invite me to share his apartment with him. It's really a basement room, but it's kind of cute. He is a very fine boy and we have fallen deeply in love and are planning to get married. We haven't got the exact date yet, but it will be before my pregnancy begins to show.

Yes, Mother and Dad, I am pregnant. I know how much you are looking forward to being grandparents and I know you will welcome the baby and give it the same love and devotion and tender care you gave me when I was a child. The reason for the delay in our marriage is the my boyfriend has a minor infection which prevents us from passing our premarital blood tests and I carelessly caught it from him.

I know that you will welcome him into our family with open arms. He is kind and, although not well educated, he is ambitious. Although he is of a different race and religion than ours, I know your often-expressed tolerance will not permit you to be bothered by that.

Now that I have brought you up to date, I want to tell you that there was no dormitory fire, I did not have a concussion or skull fracture, I was not in the hospital, I am not pregnant, I am not engaged, I am not infected, and there is no boyfriend in my life. However, I am getting a D in history and an F in science, and I want you to see these marks in their proper perspective.

Your loving daughter,

Susie

Writer Unknown.

SECTION TWO

CULTURE AND ME

If people who do not understand each other at least understand that they do not understand each other, then they understand each other better than when, not understanding each other, they do not even understand that they do not understand each other.

Gustav Ischheiser
APPEARANCES AND REALITIES

If anthropologist Edward Hall was correct when he stated "We are all captives of culture," then we need to examine how culture affects our behavior and who we are. This section provides a variety of ways for uncovering the pervasiveness of culture in our own lives.

Everyone has an ethnic heritage. Today, many students feel they have no cultural background. This simply is not true. It is important for every student to be aware of the pervasive, if often hidden, influence of culture on each and every person's experience, orientation, and perspective on life.

We live in a global society that is increasingly diverse and varied. It is essential that young people become more aware of how culture makes them who they are and how these influences affect their relationships within the many different cultural groups that make up our society today.

Some of the activities in this section will place students in differing cultural contexts. They will be asked to state how they feel about themselves and others in these contexts. Time should be provided to analyze both the conscious and unconscious behaviors that make up cultural identity and practice. There will be opportunities to examine one's own culture as seen from other vantage points. What may be assumed as logical behavior to one student may be very illogical to another.

The overall purpose of this section is to provide an experience base for examining cultural differences, how these differences make each of us who we are, and how students react to these differences in themselves and in others. This experience base is necessary to reinforce the process of perception that is examined in Section One. Students can begin to understand how their culture and that of others operates within themselves and between them.

Introduction

There is no more amorphous term used in social science than the word "culture." In various ways it has been used to mean the sum total of all the achievements, activities, customs, and attainments of any specific time period or group of people, including their arts, crafts, religion, language, agriculture, economics, beliefs, traditions, and heritage. It includes dimensions of many aspects of human behavior.

In the context of these materials, the important thing about culture is the way it is used to indicate human differences. When we talk about this culture or that culture, we are usually referring to a group or groups of people that we believe are <u>significantly</u> different from us.

This introductory activity can be used to bring out preconceived notions about what culture means. (It doesn't matter whether the group formulates a specific definition of the term.) What does matter is that students see that the term is one way humans have of seeing differences among themselves, and that we are all members of cultural groups, whether they be ethnic, gender, age, or class-based.

Objectives

Students will be able to:

- Identify the characteristics that make one group distinct from another.
- Determine one's own particular culture and how it differs from another.

Grade Level

7-12

Time

One class period

Materials

Chalkboard and chalk, OR
Butcher paper and marking pen

Procedure

1. Ask students to name as many cultural groups as they can. As they name these groups, list them on the chalkboard or paper. Some students may ask you for a definition of culture or cultural group. Explain that there is no "hard and fast" definition and that the purpose of the activity is to find out what participants think culture is.

2. After listing a number of groups, ask what makes these groups different from each other. List these characteristics on the chalkboard or paper. (Such a list might include language, religion, customs, national origin, physical features, arts and crafts, etc.)

3. After students have mentioned as many distinguishing characteristics as they can think of, ask which of the characteristics apply to all of the groups. For example, are all of the groups identifiable by different languages? Different religions? Participants should see that very few, if any, of the characteristics apply to all of the groups listed.

4. Ask:

- Why is it difficult to state a concrete definition of culture? (Because the characteristics we use to denote cultural differences are not universally applicable.)

- Why do we identify cultures and cultural groups? (Reasons will vary on this, but an important point students should raise is that such identification is a way of indicating that groups of people are different from each other.)

- Ask if any people in the group are members of any of the groups they have mentioned. Which ones? If not, which cultural groups do they consider themselves members? Would they prefer other terms such as ethnic group, racial group, nationality group, or no label at all? Why?

- What does it mean to you to say that you are a member of a particular group? (Many things, but, again, it is a way of saying that you, as a member of that group, are different in some ways from people in other groups.)

Introduction

A major first step in awareness of the diversity of ethnic groups is to examine one's own attitudes and opinions. This activity is designed to help students identify the attitudes and beliefs they hold about ethnic groups in the community and school.

Objectives

Students will be able to:

- Help increase awareness of diverse ethnic groups in the school and community.
- Understand the sources of opinions and beliefs held about these groups.
- Identify criteria used to determine ethnic group membership and affiliation.

Grade Level

5-12

Time

One class period

Materials

None

Procedure

1. Ask students to individually make a list of the various ethnic groups they know about in the school and in the community. They should try to name at least five or six different ethnic groups.

2. Have students discuss the names of ethnic groups they identified and why they listed each group as an identifiable ethnic group. As students name ethnic groups, list them on the chalkboard.

3. As names are placed on the chalkboard, ask students to discuss some of the stereotypes that are held about these ethnic groups.

4. Ask students to try to recall where these stereotypes, whether positive or negative, came from. Do they believe these stereotypes are true of the particular ethnic group? What evidence do they have to support these beliefs? Do they have any recent experiences that confirm or contradict these stereotypes or opinions about the various ethnic groups listed.

Follow-up

Divide students into small groups and have each group choose one or two of the ethnic groups listed on the chalkboard to analyze for the components that give each one specific identity as an ethnic group, or ethnic minority group. Use the definitions presented in the introduction of the unit to help students define what characteristics influenced them to name specific ethnic groups, i.e., African or Black Americans, Chicano or Hispanic Americans. Further, discuss the various labels for an ethnic group, i.e., Mexican, Chicano, Hispanic, Latin and Americans.

Introduction

Expanding on the discussions of the previous activity, this activity helps students to further explore where their attitudes about various ethnic groups originated. Students learn about people in their classes at school, but more directly, they learn about other people from their families and their experiences in the neighborhood and community.

Objectives

Students will be able to:

• Stimulate exploration of early family influences on attitudes and stereotypes of diverse ethnic groups.
• Examine the relevance of these attitudes upon current beliefs and opinions.
• Recognize the wide diversity of human nature and people's customs, traditions and practices, while understanding that all ways can be equally valid and meaningful to the ethnic group which follows that particular tradition or heritage.

Grade Level

5-12

Time

One class period

Material

Handout #13, "Questionnaire"

Procedure

1. Distribute Handout #13 and have students complete it. List various ethnic groups on the chalkboard.

2. After completing the questionnaire, divide students into small groups and have students discuss their responses. Have the small groups reach some conclusions, and then share them with the whole class.

Follow-up

Help students to recognize if their attitudes or stereotypes about various ethnic groups originated with their families. Highlight reactions of students who seem to have changed their opinions about ethnic groups, and why this change came about.

QUESTIONNAIRE

Think about a specific ethnic group that we have listed on the chalkboard and write down your reactions to these statements using these groups.

1. When I was younger _____ were seen as _____
_____.

2. I remember that in my family _____ were talked about as _____
_____.

3. The amount of actual contact my family did have with _____
was_____.

4. But now my views about _____ are (similar?, different?)
because _____
_____.

5. I would want to tell other people that _____ are
_____
_____.

Introduction

Why study ethnicity? Ethnicity may be important because we live in a neighborhood where people practice ethnic customs and beliefs. It may be important to understand why some groups of people dislike other groups of people. You might conclude that ethnicity is not very important in your own life, but that it is in the lives of others. Hence, understanding ethnicity can help us understand those around us. In this activity, students are given a questionnaire to help determine how much ethnicity means to them.

Objectives

Students will be able to:

• Recognize ethnicity in one's personal and family life.
• Recognize the factors that determine ethnic affiliation and identity.
• Be aware of the power of culture in our daily lives.

Grade Level

5-12

Time

Two to three class periods

Materials

Handout #14, "Ethnicity In My Life"
Handout #15, "Conclusions"

Procedure

1. Pass out copies of Handouts #14 and #15 and ask students to take them home with them to fill out as completely as they can. It may help to have a relative help them with some of the questions.

2. Have students bring the completed handouts back to class. Either in small groups or with the class as a whole, discuss the following:

• Compare your answers on Handout #15 with others in your class. How would you explain the fact that other students have different responses to the questions?

• Which questions do you feel would tell you the most about your own ethnicity? About someone else's ethnicity?

• Do you find that you are less concerned or more concerned about your ethnic affiliation than are your parents? Other relatives?

• How would you account for the different feelings about ethnicity in your family? Between different cultural groups in your school?

Follow-up

Have students write a summary statement or paragraph on the following topic and share it with others in the class: WHAT MY ETHNICITY MEANS TO ME.

©CTIR
University of Denver

ETHNICITY IN MY LIFE

Place a check mark (✓) by the items which you feel apply to you:

_____ 1. I attend the same church my parents attend.

_____ 2. My parents attend the same church their grandparents attend(ed).

_____ 3. I dress differently than other kids in my school.

_____ 4. I celebrate certain holidays that the majority of people in our country do not.

_____ 5. I speak our language with a heavy accent.

_____ 6. My religion requires that I not celebrate certain holidays in our nation.

_____ 7. I would prefer to marry someone of my own religious and/or ethnic group.

_____ 8. Everyone in my home speaks English as their predominant language.

_____ 9. At least one of my parents came to this country from another country.

_____10. At least one of my grandparents came to this country from another country.

_____11. In my family, we practice customs I would consider different from those of most people in this country.

_____12. My family feels that it is important that we attend events and ceremonies related to our national/religious background.

_____13. We live in the city and neighborhood we do because we share certain customs and beliefs with those around us.

_____14. I frequently speak two languages during the same day.

_____15. It is important for me and my family to socialize with people who have similar backgrounds.

_____16. I feel it is important to keep family traditions alive.

_____17. I feel it is important to use another language besides English.

_____18. I would like to visit the country my family came from more than any other foreign country.

_____19. It bothers me when other people make fun of another group's customs and language.

_____20. I belong to a club or organization that is related to my family's religious, ethnic or national background.

_____21. I was born in the this country.

_____22. My family has always spoken English.

_____23. My family name has always been the same, even generations ago.

CONCLUSIONS

Based on your responses to Handout #14 and your discussion with your parents or oth
relatives, answer the questions below.

1. I am a member of a family with strong religious-language-social-customs ties. (If s
write down what each of these ties is, e.g., religious = Catholic; language = Spanish; social
live in the same neighborhood as others in our group; customs = dress as do members of o
religious, social group.)

_____

_____

_____

_____

_____

2. The ties my family has are very important to me. Why, why not?

_____

_____

_____

_____

_____

3. The emphasis on ethnic groups and on differences among peoples is dangerous. I feel v
should all try to forget our cultural and ethnic differences and recognize ourselves
citizens of this country first. Do you agree or disagree? Explain your answer.

_____

_____

_____

_____

4. I feel that participating in events, practicing customs, and keeping my ties to an ethn
group are very important and have little or nothing to do with my being a good citizen. I
you agree or disagree? Explain your answer.

_____

_____

_____

_____

_____

5. Recently, I have become more aware of my ethnic background and would like to find out more. Agree _____ Disagree_____

6. The subject of ethnicity is not important to me at this time.
Agree _____ Disagree _____

71

Introduction

In recent years, a great deal of attention has been given to ethnic heritage and its role in a personal identity. Until the late 1960s, one could almost conclude that paying attention to ethnic differences had negative implications. "We are all Americans underneath the surface" might describe this general climate of the times. Placing emphasis on ethnic differences was often viewed as undermining the development of national character. With the emergence of the civil rights movement in the 1960s came a renewed focus on the importance of one's ethnic identity as part of total personal identity.

This activity involves students in assessing the role of ethnicity in their lives by asking them what labels they might apply to themselves. Many students may find that ethnic labels are inappropriate for them, at least initially. Moreover, as part of ethnic identity, students can see how the labels they apply to themselves compare with those applied to them by others. Finally, this activity asks, what does it mean when we refer to someone by using an ethnic label?

Objectives

Students will be able to:

• Determine a label or labels that would apply to themselves.
• Compare self-identification labels with labels used by others.
• Recognize the tendency of humans to see their own groups as different from each other, and members of other groups as similar to each other.

Grade Levels

5-12

Time

One class period

Materials

Handout #16, "Labels and Me"

Procedure

1. Distribute Handout #16 and ask students to rank the labels they think apply to them. In other words, in order of importance to each student, they are to place a "1" by the label they believe most appropriately describes them, a "2" by the label of second-most importance to them, and so on. There are, of course, no right or wrong answers in this activity. If students find that a particular label means as much or as little as another label, that is fine.

2. Ask students to answer the three questions at the bottom of the handout.

3. Have students share their answers to questions 1 and 2 on the handout with others in the class. This step should be completely voluntary.

4. Have a class discussion and ask:

- Do all of you identify yourselves in the same way? How do you account for the different labels used?

- How many of you label yourselves primarily according to ethnic group? Why do you suppose this is true?

- What does it mean when you refer to someone with a label? (Generally, it means you are referring to them in accordance with a perceived set of significant differences. They are recognizable because of these differences and are labeled accordingly.)

LABELS AND ME

On your own, rank the following labels according to their importance in your life. For example, if you feel it's most important to identify yourself as a unique individual, place the number "1" in the space in front of that label. If you would identify yourself as a teenager second, place a "2" in front of that label. If you feel labels should not be important at all in your life, place an "X" by the item "prefer no label for myself."

_____ American

_____ Catholic

_____ Protestant

_____ Jewish

_____ Other religious groups?

(Identify) _____

_____

_____

_____

_____ Student

_____ Athlete

_____ Black

_____ White

_____ Mexican American

_____ African-American

_____ Chicano(a)

_____ Hispanic

_____ Spanish American

_____ Irish American

_____ Oriental

_____ Native American

_____ Other racial group? (Identify)

_____

_____ Other ethnic group? (Identify)

_____

_____ Teenager

_____ My given name

_____ Male

_____ Human being

_____ Female

_____ I prefer no label for myself

_____ Labels other than those listed

(Identify) _____

_____ Unique individual

1. Most importantly, I call myself

_____

2. I think others would primarily label me

_____

3. What do you think it means when you refer to somebody else by a label?

_____

_____

Introduction

This questionnaire is intended as a self-inventory of feelings about certain groups in our society. It is an adaptation of the scale first developed by E. S. Bogardus to measure social distance. The term social distance refers to people's attitudes about how intimate or removed they feel from an ethnic or cultural group.

Objective

Students will be able to:

• Become aware of personal feelings about a particular group.

Grade Level

7-12

Time

One class period

Materials

Handout #17, "Questionnaire"

Procedure

1. Place the name of a cultural group in the blank provided at the top of Handout #17 (the group cannot be the one to which a student belongs).

2. Distribute a copy of the handout to each student. Let them respond to the forty statements individually. Explain to them that this exercise is intended to be a confidential self-inventory of attitudes and feelings.

3. If you should decide to have the students share some of their information with other people in the group, here is a suggested procedure:

Have students volunteer their responses to certain selected questions in the survey. Then ask:

• Are there significant differences in your responses and those of others in the group? If so, how do you account for the differences?

QUESTIONNAIRE

Directions: The following list of sentences expresses various attitudes toward a cultural group. Please read each of the statements below and indicate your feelings about each statement by placing an (x) in the column which most closely matches your reaction. Your answers will remain anonymous. The letters at the top of the columns mean:

SA   strongly agree
A   agree
U   undecided
D   disagree
SD   strongly disagree

I think _____

	SA	A	U	D	SD
1. have too many irritating habits and manners.					
2. are similar in behavior to other people.					
3. have superior athletic ability.					
4. will seek to exploit others.					
5. must be dealt with forcefully since democratic procedures will never make them behave properly.					
6. tend to keep to themselves and are suspicious of others.					
7. usually meddle too much and interfere with other people's business.					
8. are generally tolerant of other people.					

I think _____

	SA	A	U	D	SD
9. are usually intolerant of other people and new ideas.					
10. often lack initiative and dependability.					
11. are extremely ambitious, capable,a nd intelligent.					
12. are lazy and ignorant.					
13. are morally superior to others.					
14. discriminate against others.					
15. usually became wealthy by manipulating and cheating unsuspecting people.					
16. are satisfield with their lot and fair in their dealing with others.					
17. are never satisfied and are always seeking more money and power.					
18. usually try to exert control and influence over others.					
19. are behind the Communist menace in the United States.					
20. will always remain a foreign and alien element.					

I think _____

	SA	A	U	D	SD
21. have money and power out of proportion to their numbers.					
22. are mostly patriotic individuals.					
23. place foreign loyalties above patriotism and love of country.					
24. must be prevented from moving into certain neighborhoods.					
25. put more emphasis on material than spiritual values.					
26. are fair with each other but ruthless in their dealings with other people.					
27. will more than likely succeed in education.					
28. prove to be as trustworthy as other people.					
29. should be permitted to live in any neighborhood.					
30. control most of our powerful economic and political institutions.					
31. should be allowed to intermarry with any group.					
32. fail to keep up their personal appearances and neighborhoods.					

I think _____

	SA	A	U	D	SD
33. are as friendly as other people.					
34. practice strange customs.					
35. lack imagination.					
36. are very sociable.					
37. are cunning and proud.					
38. will often display compassion for people in trouble.					
39. display efficiency in most things.					
40. are often too emotional.					

Introduction

As students may have inferred from their work in Section 2 of the unit, all of us participate in activities that are directly connected with our family heritage. Many of these activities are a part of tradition and are important in determining who we are. Ethnic factors play an important role here too. The way we practice our religion, how we get married, what sports we enjoy, foods we eat, and how we entertain ourselves are affected by our ethnic affiliations.

In this activity students share these experiences with other students in the class, demonstrating the role of ethnic heritage in their social activities.

Objectives

Students will be able to:

• Participate in an experience with other students that reflects one's ethnic heritage.
• Document the relationship between ethnicity and social and/or religious activities.

Grade Level

5-12

Time

One to two class periods

Materials

Handout #18, "Which Differences Matter To Me?"

Procedure

1. Have students choose a partner or partners with whom they feel at ease.

2. Distribute Handout #18. Have students choose at least one event in which to participate from among the ethnic experiences listed in the handout.

3. Make arrangements to observe and/or participate in the event. Check with local newspapers, events calendars, etc. to make the arrangements.

4. Have students discuss the following after they have attended and observed the event:

• How did you feel while you were observing the event or ceremony?

• Were you asked, in any way, to participate? How did you react to the suggestion?

• If you attended more than one event, which did you find most unfamiliar to you? Which was most familiar to you? Why?

- How was the event similar or different from activities in your life?

- Would you be interested in going out again and attending another of the items listed? Explain.

Evaluation   Have students make a scrapbook or write an essay about the event or ceremony and feelings toward the occasion.

WHICH DIFFERENCES MATTER TO ME?

Following is a suggested list of ethnic experiences. Choose at least one; two or three would be even better:

Marriage: Wedding ceremonies, bridal showers, parties, or receptions.

Funerals: Church or funeral home service, graveside service, Irish Wake, Indian burial ceremony, or cremation.

Other Religious Ceremonies: Synagogue service, mass, church services, Bible-prayer meeting, Mormon service.

Special Religious Ceremonies: Protestant baptism, Catholic baptism, Jewish circumcision, Christian confirmations, Bar and Bat Mitzvahs.

Schools: Look in the yellow pages for types of schools in your community--Catholic, Greek, Seventh-day Adventist, Hebrew, etc.

Ethnic Holidays: Chinese New Year (Hsin Nien), St. Patrick's Day, May Day, Trung Thu, Pesadas, Cinco de Mayo, Tet, Custer Day, Sham al-Nessim, Tango-No Sekku, The Asking Festival, July 4th, the Hopi Kachina dances, Martin Luther King Day.

Ceremonies of Ethnic or Religious Organizations: Japanese Association, Sons of Italy, Masonic Order, Eastern Star, Job's Daughters, B'nai B'rith, NAACP, church youth groups, Knights of Columbus, Danish Brotherhood, St. Peter Claver Society, DeMolay.

LOOK IN YOUR LOCAL NEWSPAPER AND CHECK FOR SPECIAL ETHNIC EVENTS IN YOUR COMMUNITY.

THE ABOVE LIST IS ONLY MEANT TO SUGGEST THE KINDS OF EXPERIENCES YOU CAN OBSERVE.

Introduction

In the course of examining ethnic and cultural attitudes, many people find new or renewed interest in their own heritage. Moreover, understanding one's own heritage often complements awareness of the importance of culture and tradition to others. "If my cultural and family background is important to me, so must others treasure their backgrounds as well." This activity provides some guidelines for inquiring into one's family and cultural background.

Objective

Students will be able to:

• Ascertain the important aspects of one's culture.

Grade Level

5-12

Time

Varies

Materials

Handout #19, "Family Search and Research"

Procedure

1. Distribute copies of Handout #19 to students. Read and discuss the questions as a group.

2. Tell students to look into as many of the questions as they wish.

3. Ask:

• Is ethnicity important to you? Why? Give examples.

• Do you think it might be important to others? Why? Give examples.

FAMILY SEARCH AND RESEARCH

1. What is the origin of your family surname? What is its meaning? What, if any, changes did your family surname undergo if your ancestors came from the "old country" to this country? What stories do you know about the changes?

2. What traditional names have been used in your family? Nicknames? Are there any naming traditions?

3. What traditions have been handed down to you from branches of your family? What traditions seem to be dominant in your family's history?

4. What stories have been passed on to you about your parents? Grandparents? Ancestors? What do you know about your parents and other ancestors' childhood, religion, politics, schooling, marriage, courtship, leisure activities, attitudes about death, etc.? Are there things about your family's history you would like to know about but are afraid to ask, or about which no one seems to want to talk?

5. Is there a famous or notorious person in your family's past? What can you tell about him/her?

6. How did your parents, grandparents, great grandparents, etc., come to meet and marry? Are there family stories about these relationships (e.g., jilted brides, brief courtships, elopements, etc.)?

7. What historical events (e.g., Depression, World War I, World War II, Vietnam War, etc.) affected your family the most?

8. Are there any special family recipes that have been preserved and handed down from generation to generation in your family? Are they still in use today?

9. Are reunions held among members of your family? How often? When and where? Who's invited? Who comes? Who organizes the reunions? Are there traditional foods and activities? Are stories and photographs exchanged? Are records of the reunions kept? Are there relatives you are happy to see during these reunions? Ones that you're not so happy to see?

10. What languages have been important in your family's past and present? Religion and religious practices? Ties to a "homeland?"

©CTIR
University of Denver

Introduction   The purpose of this reading is to provide students with an example of how dominant Anglo-American societal values might appear from other vantage points. Horace Miner's essay presents an interesting, amusing perspective on many values assumed to be logical in our own society. This selection illustrates Jose Ortega y Gasset's point that reality is composed of "an infinite number of perspectives, all equally veracious and authentic. The sole false perspective is that which claims to be the only one there is."

Objective   Students will be able to:

• Objectively examine the characteristics of their own culture.

Grade Level   9-12

Time   One to two class periods

Materials   Handout #20, "Body Ritual Among the Nacirema"

Procedure   1. Have students read Handout #20.

Ask:

• What do you think were the major points of this selection?

• Miner seems to believe that culture is relative and that what is "logical" is based on cultural interpretation. Do you agree? Are there universal values that transcend cultures, in your opinion? If so, what are they?

©CTIR
University of Denver

BODY RITUAL AMONG THE NACIREMA*

The anthropologist has become so familiar with the diversity of ways in which different peoples behave in similar situations that he is not apt to be surprised by even the most exotic customs. In fact, if all of the logically possible combinations of behavior have not been found somewhere in the world, he is apt to suspect that they must be present in some yet undescribed tribe. This point has, in fact, been expressed with respect to clan organization by Murdock (1949:71). In this light, the magical beliefs and practices of the Nacirema present such unusual aspects that it seems desirable to describe them as an example of the extremes to which human behavior can go.

Professor Linton first brought the ritual of the Nacirema to the attention of anthropologists 20 years ago (1936:326), but the culture of this people is still very poorly understood. They are a North American group living in the territory between the Canadian Cree, the Yaqui and Tarahumare of Mexico, and the Carib and Arawak of the Antilles. Little is known of their origin, although tradition states that they come from the east. According to Nacirema mythology, their nation was originated by a culture hero, Notgnihsaw, who is otherwise known for two great feats of strength--the throwing of a piece of wampum across the river Pa-To-Mac and the chopping down of a cherry tree in which the Spirit of Truth resided.

Nacirema culture is characterized by a highly developed market economy which has evolved in a rich natural habitat. While much of the people's time is devoted to economic pursuits, a large part of the fruits of these labors and a considerable portion of the day are spent in ritual activity. The focus of this activity is the human body, the appearance and health of which loom as a dominant concern in the ethos of the people. While such a concern is certainly not unusual, its ceremonial aspects and associated philosophy are unique.

The fundamental belief underlying the whole system appears to be that the human body is ugly and that its natural tendency is to debility and disease. Incarcerated in such a body, man's only hope is to avert these characteristics through the use of the powerful influences of ritual and ceremony. Every household has one or more shrines devoted to this purpose. The more powerful individuals in the society have several shrines in their houses and, in fact, the opulence of a house is often referred to in terms of the number of such ritual centers it possesses. Most houses are of wattle and daub construction, but the shrine rooms of the more wealthy are walled with stone. Poorer families imitate the rich by applying pottery plaques to their shrine walls.

While each family has at least one such shrine, the rituals associated with it are not family ceremonies but are private and secret. The rites are normally only discussed with children, and then only during the period when they are being initiated into these mysteries. I was able, however, to establish sufficient rapport with the natives to examine these shrines and to have the rituals described to me.

---

*Horace Miner, "Body Ritual among the Nacirema," THE AMERICAN ANTHROPOLOGIST 58 (1956), pp 503-507. Copyright 1956 American Anthropological Association. Reprinted by permission of American Anthropological Association.

The most important part of the shrine is a box or chest which is built into the wall. In this chest are kept the many charms and magical potions without which no native believes he could live. The natives get the charms and potions from specialized practitioners. The most powerful of these are the medicine men, whose assistance must be rewarded with generous gifts. However, the medicine men do not provide the curing potions for their clients, but decide what the ingredients should be and write them down in an ancient and secret language. This writing is understood only by the medicine men and the herbalists who, for another gift, provide the required charm.

The charm is not disposed of after it has served its purpose, but is placed in the charm-box of the household shrine. As these magical materials are specific for certain ills, and the real or imagined maladies of the people are many, the charm-box is usually full to overflowing. The magical packets are so numerous that people forget what their purposes were and fear to use them again. While the natives are very vague on this point, we can only assume that the idea in retaining all the old magical materials is that their presence in the charm-box, before which the body rituals are conducted, will in some way protect the worshiper.

Beneath the charm-box is a small font. Each day every member of the family in succession enters the shrine room, bows his head before the charm-box, mingles different sorts of holy water in the font, and proceeds with a brief rite of ablution. (The holy waters are secured from the Water Temple of the community, where the priests conduct elaborate ceremonies to make the liquid ritually pure.)

In the hierarchy of magical practitioners, below the medicine men in prestige, are specialists whose designation is best translated "holy-mouth-men." The Nacirema have an almost pathological horror of and fascination with the mouth, the condition of which is believed to have a supernatural influence on all social relationships. Were it not for the rituals of the mouth, they believe that their teeth would fall out, their gums bleed, their jaws shrink, their friends desert them, and their lovers reject them. They also believe that a strong relationship exists between oral and moral characteristics. For example, there is a ritual ablution of the mouth for children which is supposed to improve their moral fiber.

The daily body ritual performed by everyone includes a mouth-rite. Despite the fact that these people are so punctilious about care of the mouth, this rite involves a practice which strikes the uninitiated stranger as revolting. It was reported to me that the ritual consists of inserting a small bundle of hog hairs into the mouth, along with certain magical powders, and then moving the bundle in a highly formalized series of gestures.

In addition to the private mouth-rite, the people seek out a holy-mouth-man once or twice a year. These practitioners have an impressive set of paraphernalia, consisting of a variety of augers, awls, probes, and prods. The use of these objects in the exorcism of the evils of the mouth involves almost unbelievable ritual torture of the client. The holy-mouth-man opens the client's mouth and, using the above-mentioned tools, enlarges any holes which decay may have created in the teeth. Magical materials are put into these holes. If there are no naturally occurring holes in the teeth, large sections of one or more teeth are gouged out so that the supernatural substances can be applied. In the client's view, the purpose of these ministrations is to arrest decay and to draw friends. The extremely sacred and traditional character of the rite is evident in the fact that the natives return to the holy-mouth-man year after year, despite the fact that their teeth continue to decay.

It is to be hoped that, when a thorough study of the Nacirema is made, there will be careful inquiry into the personality structure of these people. One has but to watch the gleam in the eye of a holy-mouth-man, as he jabs an awl into an exposed nerve, to suspect that a certain amount of sadism is involved. If this can be established, a very interesting pattern emerges, for most of the population shows definite masochistic tendencies. It was to these that Professor Linton referred in discussing a distinctive part of the daily body ritual which is performed only by men. This part of the rite involves scraping and lacerating the surface of the face with a sharp instrument. Special women's rites are performed only four times during each lunar month, but what they lack in frequency is made up in barbarity. As part of this ceremony, women bake their heads in small ovens for about an hour. The theoretically interesting point is that in what seems to be a preponderantly masochistic people have developed sadistic specialists.

The medicine men have an imposing temple, or latipso, in every community of any size. The more elaborate ceremonies required to treat very sick patients can only be performed at this temple. These ceremonies involve not only the thaumaturge but a permanent group of vestal maidens who move sedately about the temple chambers in distinctive costume and headdress.

The latipso ceremonies are so harsh that it is phenomenal that a fair proportion of the really sick natives who enter the temple ever recover. Small children whose indoctrination is still incomplete have been known to resist attempts to take them to the temple because "that is where you go to die." Despite this fact, sick adults are not only willing but eager to undergo the protracted ritual purification, if they can afford to do so. No matter how ill the supplicant or how grave the emergency, the guardians of many temples will not admit a client if he cannot give a rich gift to the custodian. Even after one has gained admission and survived the ceremonies, the guardians will not permit the neophyte to leave until he makes still another gift.

The supplicant entering the temple is first stripped of all his or her clothes. In everyday life the Nacirema avoids exposure of his body and its natural functions. Bathing and excretory acts are performed only in the secrecy of the household shrine, where they are ritualized as part of the body rites. Psychological shock results from the fact that body secrecy is suddenly lost upon entry into the latipso. A man whose own wife has never seen him in an excretory act suddenly finds himself naked and assisted by a vestal maiden while he performs his natural functions into a sacred vessel. This sort of ceremonial treatment is necessitated by the fact that the excreta are used by a diviner to ascertain the course and nature of the client's sickness. Female clients, on the other hand, find their naked bodies are subjected to the scrutiny, manipulation, and prodding of the medicine men.

Few supplicants in the temple are well enough to do anything but lie on their hard beds. The daily ceremonies, like the rites of the holy-mouth-man, involve discomfort and torture. With ritual precision, the vestals awaken their miserable charges each dawn and roll them about on their beds of pain while performing ablutions, in the formal movements of which the maidens are highly trained. At other times they insert magic wands in the applicant's mouth or force him to eat substances which are supposed to be healing. From time to time the medicine men come to their clients and jab magically treated needles into their flesh. The fact that these temple ceremonies may not cure, and may even kill the neophyte, in no way decreases the people's faith in the medicine men.

There remains one other kind of practitioner, known as a "listener." This witch doctor has the power to exorcise the devils that lodge in the heads of people who have been bewitched. The Nacirema believe that parents bewitch their own children. Mothers are particularly suspected of putting a curse on children while teaching them the secret body rituals. The counter magic of the with doctor is unusual in its lack of ritual. The patient simply tells the "listener" all his troubles and fears, beginning with the earliest difficulties he can remember. The memory displayed by the Nacirema is these exorcism sessions is truly remarkable. It is not uncommon for the patient to bemoan the rejection he felt being weaned as a babe, and a few individuals even see their troubles going back to the traumatic effects of their own birth.

In conclusion, mention must be made of certain practices which have their base in native aesthetics but which depend upon the pervasive aversion to the natural body and its functions. There are ritual fasts to make fat people thin and ceremonial feat to make thin people fat. Still other rites are used to make women's breasts large if they are small, and smaller if they are large. General dissatisfaction with breast shape is symbolized in the fact that the ideal form is virtually outside the range of human variation. A few women afflicted with almost inhuman hypermammary development are so idolized that they make a handsome living by simply going from village to village and permitting the natives to stare at them for a fee.

Reference has already been made to the fact that excretory functions are ritualized, routinized, and relegated to secrecy. Natural reproductive functions are similarly distorted. Intercourse is taboo as a topic and scheduled as an act. Efforts are made to avoid pregnancy by the use of magical material or by limiting intercourse to certain phases of the moon. Conception is actually very infrequent. When pregnant, women dress so as to hide their condition. Parturition takes place in secret, without friends or relatives to assist, and majority of the women do not nurse their infants.

Our review of the ritual life of the Nacirema has certainly shown them to be a magic-ridden people. It is hard to understand how they have managed to exist so long under the burdens which they have imposed upon themselves. But even such exotic customs as these take on real meaning when they are viewed with the insight provided by Malinowski when he wrote (1948:70):

> Looking from far and above, from our high places of safety in the developed civilization, it is easy to see all the crudity and irrelevance of magic. But without its power and guidance early man could not have mastered his practical difficulties as he has done, nor could man have advanced to the higher stages of civilization.

Introduction

It has been estimated that about 90 percent of human communication is nonverbal. Such an estimate suggests that it is probably as important to understand the cultural and ethnic variations in behavior, customs, and manners as it is to learn another group's language or dialect. Understanding and adjusting to these variations can mean the difference between successful and unsuccessful intercultural communication.

The following set of roleplays is designed to help students check out their reactions to variations in nonverbal behavior and to look into the function of nonverbal communication in cultural awareness.

Objective

Students will be able to:

• Recognize the importance of nonverbal communication.

Grade Level

3-12

Time

One class period

Materials

Handout #21 "Cronies"
Handout #22, "Ords"
Handout #23, "Fondis"
Handout #24, "Dandis"
Handout #25, "Lindis"

Procedure

1. Divide the class into groups of four. Preferably, each pair in the foursome should consist of a male and a female, although this is not absolutely necessary for a successful experience. Look through the five sets of roleplaying situations and choose one or two for each group to do. (Note: each roleplaying situation consists of two sheets, A and B.)

2. Explain that the goal of the activity is to learn more about the variety of human behavior that influences communication between cultures.

3. Give one pair of students in the foursome one of the sheets marked B. Instruct the pair to leave the room, study their roles for about five minutes, and be ready to return to the room when called upon to do so.

4. Give the other pair in the foursome the sheet marked A. Instruct them to read and study their roles and be ready to meet the B pair in their foursome in a few minutes. Explain to the rest of the class that they are to act as observers by noting what specific behaviors are demonstrated by both of the pairs in the roleplay.

5. Bring the two pairs together and ask them to proceed with the roleplay. Each situation should take no longer then ten to fifteen minutes to act out.

6. After each group has acted out their roleplay, hold a class discussion.

- Were the "foreigners" able to accomplish their task? What accounts for their being able or not being able to accomplish the task?

- How did the students who roleplayed the situation with the Ords feel about their respective roles? Were they comfortable or uncomfortable? Was it difficult for the Ords to act out their roles? Why do you suppose many people feel uncomfortable touching members of the same sex?

- How did the foursome who roleplayed the situation with the Dandis feel while acting out their roles? Why do you suppose many people might have difficulty in physically standing so close to others? (Point out examples: In many Latin American and West Asian societies, there are different views about proximity.) Can students think of examples of body space differences based on their own intercultural and travel experiences?

- Ask for comments about how participants in the Cronies, Fondis, and Lindis situations felt about their respective roles. Were the "Americans" successful in accomplishing their goals in these situations?

- What cultural practices do we have that might seem strange or even ridiculous to some outsiders to our culture? Which ones do you think might cause difficulty in cross-cultural communication? Try to point out as many as you can. (Example: People in the United States have a concept of body space that is quite different from that found among Latin Americans. If it is a sign of warmth and friendliness to stand close to others in a Latin American context, then standing farther apart, as is usually the case among people in the U.S., might indicate to Latin Americans that they wish to be unfriendly with them.)

- Which of the customs that you saw roleplayed or participated in do you feel would cause the most difficulty in achieving successful cross-cultural communications?

- Which of the cultural practices would you feel most uncomfortable with? Most comfortable with? Which ones do you think you could change your feelings about most easily and readily?

CRONIES   A

You are two people from the land of <u>Crony</u>. As Cronies, you have certain ways of doing some things. Your land is run by <u>females</u> (girls and women). The females in your land are in charge of all the important parts of Crony life. For example, if one has an important favor to ask of someone else in Crony, a girl must ask another girl. A boy cannot ask an important favor of another boy. It is forbidden for a boy to ask a girl for a favor. When boys talk it is almost always unimportant "chit-chat." Everything important is decided by girls. All important talk is between girls.

It is very rude for anyone from another land to ask about how things are done in Crony.

You are about to meet two people from another country who are traveling through Crony. They went out on their own to find out what Crony is like and lost all their money. Now the two people are <u>stranded</u> a long distance from their hotel. They have no money for the bus which is the only way of getting back to the hotel. (There are no trains or taxis or cars or motorcycles in Crony.) There are no other people of their nationality around so they will ask you for help. Their job is to get you to loan or give them enough money for bus fare back to their hotel.

As you talk to them pretend to be Cronies. Do everything as you think Cronies would. If these people cannot figure out the correct and proper way to ask a favor of a Crony, then you should <u>not</u> give or loan them the money.

- -

CRONIES   B

You are two foreigners traveling through a land known as Crony. You went out on your own to find out what Crony is like. You both accidentally lost all your money. Now you are <u>stranded</u> fifty miles from your hotel without any bus fare. (There are no trains or taxis or cars or motorcycles in Crony.) There are no other people of your nationality around so you decide to ask two Crony citizens for help. Your job is to get the two Cronies to loan or give you enough money for bus fare back to your hotel.

You know very little about the land of Crony and how its people do things. In order to get the money you need you will have to figure out what is important in the way to ask a Crony for a favor. You probably should <u>not</u> come right out and ask how you should talk to a Crony. You might make them angry. Before you go to the Cronies, you two talk about WHAT you are going to say and HOW you are going to say it to get your bus fare.

©CTIR
University of Denver

ROLE SHEET

ORDS   A

You are two people from the land of Ord. As Ords, you have certain ways of doing some things. For one thing, touching is very important when boys talk to other boys or when girls talk to other girls. Children of Ord are raised around people who do a lot of gentle patting and hugging when they talk to other people of the same sex. When talking, boys pat and hug other boys; girls hug and pat other girls. However, this touching is never done while talking to a member of the opposite sex--when a boy and girl talk.

When talking in the land of Ord, looking right into another's eyes is very important. When boys are talking to boys or when girls are talking to girls, they must look into each other's eyes at all times. However, as with touching, when a boy and girl talk together, they **must not** look into each other's eyes.

It is very rude for anyone from another land to ask about how things are done in Ord.

You are about to meet two people from another country who are traveling through your country. They went out on their own to find out what Ord is like and lost all their money. Now the two people are <u>stranded</u> a long distance from their hotel. They have no money for the bus which is the only way of getting back to the hotel. (There are no trains or taxis or cars or motorcycles in Ord.) There are not other people of their nationality around so they will ask you for help. Their job is to get you to loan or give them enough money for bus fare back to their hotel.

As you talk to them, pretend to be Ords. Do everything as you think Ords would. If the foreigners cannot figure out the correct and proper way to ask a favor of an Ord, then you should **not** give or loan them the money.

- -

ORDS   B

You are two foreigners traveling through a land known as Ord. You went out on your own to find out what Ord is like. You both accidentally lost all your money. Now you are <u>stranded</u> fifty miles from your hotel without any bus fare. (There are no trains or taxis or cars or motorcycles in Ord.) There are no other people of your nationality around so you decide to ask two Ord citizens for help. Your job is to get the two Ords to loan or give you enough money for bus fare back to your hotel.

You know very little about the land of Ord and how its people do things. In order to get the money you need you will have to figure out what is important in the way to ask an Ord for a favor. You probably should **not** come right out and ask how you should talk to an Ord. You might make them angry. Before you go to the Ords, you two talk about WHAT you are going to say and HOW you are going to say it to get your bus fare.

©CTIR
University of Denver

FONDIS   **A**

You are two people of the land of <u>Fondi</u>. As Fondis you have certain ways of doing some things. For one thing, using the correct expression on your face when talking to others is very important. When someone says something a Fondi likes or agrees with, it is usual for the listener to look down and frown. Also, if a Fondi hears something he doesn't like or disagrees with, it is usual for the listener to smile and nod his head up and down.

Especially important to the Fondis is correct use of the hands when talking. As a Fondi, if you were to place your hands on your hips it would show that you disagreed with what someone was saying. If you agreed with what a person was saying your would put your hand in front of the other person's face with the palm toward them. There is one important thing that a Fondi should never do. A Fondi never touches his face or head in any way when he is talking. Such touching on one's face or head when talking is a terrible thing for a Fondi to do!

It is very rude for anyone from another land to ask about how things are done in Fondi.

You are about to meet two foreigners who are traveling through your country. They went out on their own to find out what Fondi is like and lost all their money. Now the two people are <u>stranded</u> a long distance from their hotel. They have no money for the bus which is the only way of getting back to the hotel. (There are no trains or taxis or cars or motorcycles in Fondi.) There are no other people of their nationality around so they will ask you for help. Their job is to get you to loan or give them enough money for bus fare back to their hotel.

As you talk to them pretend to be Fondis. Do everything as you think Fondis would. If the foreigners cannot figure out the correct and proper way to ask a favor of a Fondi, then you should <u>not</u> give or loan them the money.

- -

FONDIS   **B**

You are two foreigners traveling through a land known as Fondi. You went out on your own to find out what Fondi is like. You both accidentally lost all your money. Now you are <u>stranded</u> fifty miles from your hotel without any bus fare. (There are no trains or taxis or cars or motorcycles in Fondi.) There are no other people of your nationality around so you decide to ask two Fondi citizens for help. Your job is to get the two Fondis to loan or give you enough money for bus fare back to your hotel.

You know very little about the land or Fondi and how its people do things. In order to get the money you need you will have to figure out what is important in the way to ask a Fondi for a favor. You probably should <u>not</u> come right out and how ask you should talk to a Fondi. You might make them angry. Before you go to the Fondis, you two talk about WHAT you are going to say and HOW you are going to say it to get your bus fare.

DANDIS   A

You are two people from the land of <u>Dandi</u>. As Dandis, you have certain ways of doing some things. For one thing, all Dandis must always use their voices correctly. You have been brought up to NEVER raise your voice when talking to someone, unless you are angry.

Since everyone speaks in such soft voices in Dandi, people talking to each other stand 12 inches (one ruler-length) apart or even closer. People who stand further than 12 inches apart while talking are considered cold and standoffish.

It is very rude for anyone from another land to ask about how things are done in Dandi.

You are about to meet two foreigners who are traveling through your country. They went out on their own to find out what Dandi is like and lost all their money. Now the two people are <u>stranded</u> a long distance from their hotel. They have no money for the bus which is the only way of getting back to the hotel. (There are no trains or taxis or cars or motorcycles in Dandi.) There are no other people of their nationality around so they will ask you for help. Their job is to get you to loan or give them enough money for bus fare back to their hotel.

As you talk to them pretend to be Dandis. Do everything as you think Dandis would. If the foreigners cannot figure out the correct and proper way to ask a favor of a Dandi, then you should <u>not</u> give or loan them the money.

- -

DANDIS   B

You are two foreigners traveling through a land known as Dandi. You went out on your own to find out what Dandi is like. You both accidentally lost all your money. Now you are <u>stranded</u> fifty miles from your hotel without any bus fare. (There are no trains or taxis or cars or motorcycles in Dandi.) There are no other people of your nationality around so you decide to ask two Dandi citizens for help. Your job is to get the two Dandis to loan or give you enough money for bus fare back to your hotel.

You know very little about the land or Dandi and how its people do things. In order to get the money you need you will have to figure out what is important in the way to ask a Dandi for a favor. You probably should <u>not</u> come right out and ask how you should talk to a Dandi. You might make them angry. Before you go to the Dandis, you two talk about WHAT you are going to say and HOW you are going to say it to get your bus fare.

©CTIR
University of Denver

LINDIS   A

You are two people from the land of Lindi. As Lindis you have certain ways of doing some things. Very important among Lindis are the special ways of giving and getting loans and gifts. When a Lindi LOANS another person something, the receiver of the loan must give the lender something in return. The borrower must pay back the loan, but the lender gets to keep what was given him in return.

Gifts are never offered without the giver suggesting that he get part of the gift himself. For example, if a Lindi were to give another person a loaf of bread, he would expect to share part of the loaf himself.

The difference between lending and giving seems strange to many outsiders but it began at a time in Lindi history when loans and gifts were ruining many friendships. So the above ways of giving and lending were begun.

It is very rude for anyone from another land to ask about how things are done in Lindi.

You are about to meet two foreigners who are traveling through your country. They went out on their own to find out what Lindi is like and lost all their money. Now the two people are <u>stranded</u> a long distance from their hotel. They have no money for the bus which is the only way of getting back to the hotel. (There are no trains or taxis or cars or motorcycles in Lindi.) There are no other persons of their nationality around so they will ask you for help. Their job is to get you to loan or give them enough money for bus fare back to their hotel.

As you talk to them pretend to be Lindis. Do everything as you think Lindis would. If the foreigners cannot figure out the correct and proper way to ask a favor of a Lindi, then you should <u>not</u> give or loan them the money.

- -

LINDIS   B

You are two foreigners traveling through a land known as Lindi. You went out on your own to find out what Lindi is like. You both accidentally lost all your money. Now you are <u>stranded</u> fifty miles from your hotel without any bus fare. (There are no trains or taxis or cars or motorcycles in Lindi.) There are no other people of your nationality around so you decide to ask two Lindi citizens for help. Your job is to get the two Lindis to loan or give you enough money for bus fare back to your hotel.

You know very little about the land or Lindi and how its people do things. In order to get the money you need you will have to figure out what is important in the way to ask a Lindi for a favor. You probably should <u>not</u> come right out and ask how you should talk to a Lindi. You might make them angry. Before you go to the Lindis, you two talk about WHAT you are going to say and HOW you are going to say it to get your bus fare.

SECTION THREE

CULTURAL CONFLICT, DISCRIMINATION, AND INSTITUTIONAL RACISM

All you white folks could leave America tomorrow
. . .   leave nobody but us Blacks, Mexican Americans,
Puerto Ricans, and Indians, and, if we had to take them
same old trick tests to get into these institutions, we sti
couldn't make it.

Dick Gregory

There are no more emotionally loaded and potentially explosive topics among people than discrimination and racism. It is one thing to deal with stereotypes and prejudice. Those concepts can be intellectually dismissed as little more than hypothetical constructs, or those fuzzy things we call "attitudes." But discrimination focuses on our behavior. It represents all the distasteful manifestations of prejudice and stereotyping, everything from a storekeeper who behaves toward all Mexican Americans as if they were thieves, to the horrors of the gas ovens in Nazi Germany.

Racism is a sticky subject because people are super-sensitive to the suggestion that they might be, consciously or unconsciously, behaving in racist ways. The dynamics of racism are often the same as those found in sexist behavior or in ageism. Let's face it! To be called a racist or sexist has become about as bad as being labeled a criminal.

As distasteful as these topics might be, they must be examined. Not to deal with discrimination and racism could leave this program on cultural awareness superficial and misleading--superficial, because the real impact of differences is on how they are used to establish one group's superiority over another's; misleading, because people can be left with the impression that merely recognizing stereotypes and prejudice is enough to provide a solid foundation for change.

Such recognition is a good and necessary first step, but it is not enough. There is another dimension to cultural awareness that can help provide a firmer foundation for change. People need to recognize the subtle and ongoing ways in which society's institutions contribute to the perpetuation of inequality and cultural conflict.

This section is designed to raise consciousness about discrimination and the "isms" it produces. Legislation has removed much of the blatant forms of racism that pervaded American life for so many years. Yet, the subtle, covert kind of racist and sexist behavior persists. And, racism cannot be confronted and eradicated unless it is recognized. Perhaps the activities in this section can contribute to the fulfillment of the goal of consciousness and awareness that will lead to actions which promote fairness for all.

Introduction

This activity is a self-test relating personal beliefs to ethnic attitudes. It is based on material written by Gordon Allport.

Objectives

Students will be able to:

- Examine some characteristics of prejudice.
- Explore feelings about prejudice towards differences.
- Recognize prejudicial statements.

Grade Level

5-12

Time

One class period

Materials

Handout #26, "The Prejudiced Personality"

Procedure

1. Write the following statements on the chalkboard.

- Statement 1: "There is only one right way to do anything."
- Statement 2: "If a person does not watch out, somebody will make a sucker out of him."
- Statement 3: "It would be better if teachers would be more strict."
- Statement 4: "Only people who are like myself have a right to be happy."
- Statement 5: "Girls should learn only things that are useful around the house."
- Statement 6: "There will always be war; it is part of human nature."
- Statement 7: "The position of the stars at the time of your birth tells your character and personality."

2. Ask students to break into groups of three or four.

3. Read the following instructions to students:

On the chalkboard, you will find statements of opinion in quotation marks. For the next fifteen minutes, you and the rest of your group are to discuss which of the statements have anything to do with prejudice. Elect a spokesperson for your group. They should be ready to report the group's conclusions at the end of the 15-minute period. Jot down the number(s) of those statements the group feels has very little to do with prejudice.

4. Discuss group responses to the statements, and why or why not students feel the statements relate to prejudice.

5. Distribute copies of Handout #26.

6. Discuss students' reactions to Allport's statements.

100 ©CTIR

"THE PREJUDICED PERSONALITY"*

The exercise you've just completed might have proved helpful in sorting out elements of personality that tend to characterize prejudice. According to Gordon W. Allport, a well-known sociologist, <u>all</u> of the beliefs your group dealt with on the chalkboard describe the prejudiced personality:

According to Allport, prejudiced people tend to endorse the following beliefs:

1. There is only one right way to do anything.

2. If a person does not watch out, somebody will make a sucker out of him.

3. It would be better if teachers would be more strict.

4. Only people who are like myself have a right to be happy.

5. Girls should learn only things that are useful around the house.

6. There will always be war; it is part of human nature.

7. The position of the stars at the time of your birth tells your character and personality.

Certain types of propositions are endorsed by highly prejudiced people more often than by tolerant people:

The world is a hazardous place in which people are basically evil and dangerous.

On the whole, I am more afraid of swindlers than I am of gangsters.

Says Allport, "At first sight these propositions seem to have nothing to do with prejudice. Yet it is proved that all of them have. This finding can only mean that prejudice is frequently woven firmly into a style of life."

- -

Write your answers to the following questions on the back of this sheet or another sheet of paper.

A. Do you agree with Allport or not? Explain.

B. How yould you go about finding out whether or not <u>all</u> of the statements would apply to a prejudiced personality? Is there any way to measure? If you cannot think of a way to measure the statements in relation to prejudice, does any of the exercise really matter?

---

*Gordon W. Allport, <u>The Nature of Prejudice</u>. New York: Doubleday and Co., 1958.

101   ©CTIR

Introduction   Which groups come to mind when you think of those who have been discriminated against in our society? Many groups? A limited number? Moreover, which groups fall into categories of being victims of individual and institutional racism?

Objectives   Students will be able to:

- Identify those groups judged to be victims of discrimination.
- Classify victims into individual and/or institutional forms of racism.

Grade Level   10-12

Time   One class period

Materials   Handout #27, "A Bunch of Groups"

Procedure   1. Divide the class into groups of three students each.

2. Distribute copies of the handout to each group.

3. As the students examine the list of groups, ask them to decide with the other members of their trio how to mark the blanks to the left of each group. They should mark them according to the following:

a. If the group is one that has been or is currently discriminated against;
b. If the group is a victim of <u>individual</u> racism; or
c. If the group is a victim of <u>institutional</u> racism.

Remember, more than one answer is certainly possible in each blank.

4. Hold a class discussion and ask:

- Were you surprised at the number of times you gave responses to groups?

- Which groups seem most commonly victims of certain kinds of racism? Why?

A BUNCH OF GROUPS

_____Quakers

_____Catholics

_____Jews

_____Mormons

_____Black Muslims

_____Native Americans

_____Baptists

_____Methodists

_____Lutherans

_____Puritans

_____Atheists

_____Irish

_____Italians

_____Polish

_____Germans

_____Danes

_____Scots

_____Puerto Ricans

_____Mexicans

_____Chinese

_____Japanese

_____Blacks

_____Whites

_____Southerners

_____Northerners

_____Easterners

_____Westerners

_____Midwesterners

_____Poor people

_____Rich people

_____Union members

_____Nonunion members

_____Unemployed people

_____Lawyers

_____Doctors

_____Plumbers

_____Teachers

_____Cowboys

_____Farmers

_____Prisoners

_____Politicians

_____Journalists

_____Athletes

_____Artists

_____Beauticians

_____Police officers

_____Car mechanics

_____Car dealers

_____Forecasters

_____Poets

_____Drinkers

_____Nondrinkers

_____Smokers

_____Gamblers

_____Fat people

_____Skinny people

_____Redheads

_____Bald people

_____Old people

_____Married people

_____Divorced people

_____Single people

_____Women

_____Men

_____Teenagers

_____Children

_____Dentists

_____Nonsmokers

_____Nurses

Introduction

Prejudice is defined in Webster's New Universal Unabridged Dictionary as "a judgment or opinion formed before the facts are known, a preconceived idea." In today's world, we are all exposed to people from diverse cultures and this has created some problems that have not been faced in the past. The article in this activity discusses some of the paradoxes of prejudice that many people face in their everyday lives.

Objectives

Students will be able to:

- Define prejudice.
- Become aware of prejudice.

Grade Level

7-12

Time

One class period

Materials

Handout #28, "Paradoxes of Prejudice"

Procedure

1. Have students discuss and develop their own definition of prejudice. You can bring in Webster's definition if appropriate.

2. Distribute Handout #28 and have students read the article.

3. Hold a class discussion and ask:

- How did you feel when you read the article? Were you in agreement?

- In your environment, have you experienced or observed acts of prejudice that you felt were a result of the other person having a preconceived idea about a race instead of putting things on an individual basis?

4. Discuss with students forms of prejudice and the paradoxes that can occur. Some examples are:

- Some California universities limiting the number of Orientals admitted to their institutions.

- Hiring only Japanese gardeners because of their supposed innate gardening ability.

- Blacks are natural athletes.

- Native Americans like bright colors and are natural trackers.

Follow-up   The following statement was written by Shelby Steele, an associate professor of English at San Jose State University in California.

> **When everyone is on the run from his anxieties about race, race relations . . . can be reduced to the negotiation of avoidance.**

Ask the students to write a short response to this statement, including the paradoxes that can occur. If you feel it is appropriate, have students present their responses to the rest of the class.

PARADOXES OF PREJUDICE

You will be pleased to know--probably--that 98% of white Americans expressing an opinion would have no problem if a black family moved in next door, that 88% would have no problem if their 6-year-old child brought home a black friend, that 95% would have no problem having a black boss and that 89% would have no problem about going to a doctor who is black.

Golly, it's nice to live in such an open-minded country! And it must be so, because it's in a USA Today poll, and polls never lie.

On the other hand, you will--probably--be discomfited to know that the same survey shows that 60% of blacks believe that they encounter racial prejudice either "daily" (9%), "frequently" (13%) or "sometimes" (38%).

A further break-out of the poll shows that well-to-do blacks are much more likely to feel discriminated against than are poorer blacks. Thus, 66% of blacks earning over $50,000 feel they have been viewed as a criminal just because they are black; 79% report they receive prejudiced treatment while shopping.

It's a mystery. All those nice unprejudiced whites, and all those blacks being discriminated against. Who's doing it? The other person, that's who. Of the white respondents, 60% say they are less prejudiced than "the average person," and only 3% say they are more prejudiced.

To add to the confusion, the same poll shows that solid majorities of whites and solid pluralities of blacks believe that opportunities for blacks have improved in the past 10 years and will continue to improve in the next 10 years.

What's happening? There is progress. If the poll were taken a couple of decades ago it would probably not have bothered to dwell on upper-income blacks. There weren't many. But the USA Today story accompanying the poll quotes a black female engineer saying that store clerks "often ignore you because they feel you don't have the money. So one day I put on my mink coat, my Gucci bag and my diamond ring and walked into the store"--and then service improved. Exaggerated? sure, but that's not your standard exaggerated anecdote from yesteryear.

And there is even evidence of a form of almost perverse progress revealed by the fact that upper-income blacks feel discriminated against. That is likely coming about because as blacks move up the income ladder, there is more of the civil rights dream. But because there is still some race prejudice, it will be felt by more blacks as more contact is made, even if the prejudice itself is diminishing over time.

_____

Ben Wattenberg, September 1989. Reprinted by permission of Newspaper Enterprise Association.

©CTIR
University of Denver

There is also a form of attitudinal progress shown when white respondents are fearful to suggest, even to a pollster pledging confidentiality, that he or she may act in a prejudiced way.

Further, there may well be acts that appear racist to blacks, but not to whites. On a recent <u>Nightline</u> program, a black ABC reporter noted bitterly that even when a black had achieved status, it was hard to successfully hail a cab.

But is it racist when a black cab driver passes by a potential black fare? (And they do.) It is surely a prejudiced act. But we can also assume that a black cab driver is not acting out of race hatred. Something else is at work.

Cab drivers, blacks and whites, know that the violent crime rate among blacks is five times greater proportionally than among whites. The cab drivers, of both races, are often nervous about picking up blacks becuase they are fearful of becoming a crime statistic. Is that racism?

And so, complexity and paradox. Blacks are making headway--and finding discimination. Whites are becoming less prejudiced as time goes on--but reacting understandably to real fears.

Introduction

It is possible to identify several levels of understanding of another culture or ethnic group. Most curriculum limits itself to dealing only with intellectual understanding, if even that is achieved. We believe that materials should provide some opportunity for students to explore deeper, more affective levels of understanding. We also realize that all students may not be able to participate in the experience outlined below. But, through sharing experiences with those who were unable to participate, the activity might enhance their understanding of differences as well.

Objective

Students will be able to:

• Experience cultural differences first hand.

Grade Level

5-12

Time

Approximately one day

Materials

None

Procedure

1. Have students choose a partner of the same sex who is of a different ethnic or cultural group. (Possible pairs: Black-White; Chicano-Anglo: Irish American-Native American; first born-third born; Jewish-Protestant.)

2. After students have chosen their partners, explain:

> **Make arrangements to visit with each other for a day, or evening. You should discuss at considerable length the implications of doing so. Will you feel so out of place that the activity might do you more harm than good? Do both parents know of this experiment and approve?**

> **Spend the day or evening with your partner both in and out of the house. (You'll need to make all of the appropriate arrangements and check with parents, or other relative, for permission of course!)**

Things to look for and note:

Speak each other's <u>language</u> as much as possible, if applicable.

Wear each other's <u>clothes</u>, if possible.

Attend each other's church services, other family/cultural activities.

Learn and practice each other's customs, mannerisms, etc.

Follow each other's routines.

3. After the day's role switch, discuss the following with students:

• Were each of you comfortable with the new role you took on?

• What specific things did you learn about the other person and their group that you were unaware of at the beginning of the day?

• What specific things did you learn about yourself and your attitudes about the other person's group?

• What <u>differences</u> between your lifestyle and your partner's lifestyle did you find most difficult to deal with? Least difficult? Why? Do you think most people in similar situations would react this way? Explain.

Follow-up

Have students find a medium (written, pictures, spoken, drawing, etc.) to express their feelings about the following: MY FEELING ABOUT_____ ARE DIFFERENT NOW, BECAUSE

_____

Ask students to keep this reaction statement with them and examine it again in a few months.

Introduction   This activity has students examine their own cultural discrimination through a role play.

Objective   Students will be able to:

• Help clarify values regarding cultural discrimination.

Grade Level   5-12

Time   One class period

Materials   Handout #29, "Mr. Smith's Will"

Procedure   1. Divide the class into two groups. Separate the groups into two different rooms.

2. Distribute copies of Handout #29, the Anglo donor portion to one group and the Afro-American donor portion to the other group. Instruct each group that they have twenty minutes in which to reach group consensus on the two questions at the bottom of the slip of paper.

At this point, neither group should know that the other group has a different version. It is sufficient to tell curious students that both groups have Mr. Smith's will.

If there is a great deal of disagreement among members of the group, they can decide to issue a majority report and a minority report if desired.

At the end of the twenty minute group discussion, bring both groups together for debriefing.

3. Ask students the following, but allow students to discover for themselves that there were two different versions of Mr. Smith's will.

Which man, Mr. Smith or his lawyer, would your group side with and why?

What, if any, were some of the minority opinions within your group?

Were there significant differences in the answers between the two groups? If so, why?

What are your conclusions about the morality of what Mr. Smith did, regardless of which cultural groups are involved?

Follow-up

1. Set up a test in your community. Say at a shopping mall to determine how discrimination works. For example, are young men and young women treated differently at an electronics store? What are the differences? How do students feel about this discrimination? What can be done to change this behavior?

2. Document specific techniques of discrimination based on culture that occur in your community. How were these procedures established? What can be done to change this behavior?

©CTIR
University of Denver

MR. SMITH'S WILL

Mr. Smith is a wealthy Anglo citizen who is lying on his death-bed. Present in the bedroom is Mr. Smith's lawyer who has arrived on the scene to draft Mr. Smith's will. Mr. Smith has decided to leave his money to build a hospital that will provide free medical care for persons of African-American descent. The lawyer argues that the decision is unfair and discriminatory since it excludes members of other ethnic groups, and that it perpetuates inequality in our society.

WHICH MAN, MR. SMITH OR HIS LAWYER, WOULD YOU SIDE WITH? WHY?

MR. SMITH'S WILL

Mr. Smith is a wealthy African-American who is lying on his death-bed. Present in the bedroom is Mr. Smith's lawyer who has arrived on the scene to draft Mr. Smith's will. Mr. Smith has decided to leave his money to build a hospital that will provide free medical care for persons of African-American descent. The lawyer argues that the decision is unfair and discriminatory since it excludes members of other ethnic groups, and that it perpetuates inequality in our society.

WHICH MAN, MR. SMITH OR HIS LAWYER, WOULD YOU SIDE WITH? WHY?

Introduction   This activity is based on recent history. It's a copy of questions contained in the Alabama literacy test, required for voter registration. Until the Civil Rights Act of 1965, such tests were instituted in many southern states to keep blacks from registering to vote. (Actually, as a condition of voter registration, literacy tests were not completely eliminated until 1970.)

This is how the system worked in many counties. A black registrant would go to the registrar in his county. He would be given a test, such as the one accompanying this activity. Even though whites had to take the same test, the interpretation as to how the registrant scored was left up to the discretion of the registrar. So, a white registrant might be declared "competent to vote" simply because he filled out the test. A black registrant might be declared "incompetent to vote" simply because he missed one single question! This activity examines how racism became institutionalized in the political arena. Answers are not provided for the test because the answers are not important in understanding the test as an example of racism.

Objective   Students will be able to:

• Identify forms of institutional racism in our society today.

Grade Level   7-12

Time   One class period

Materials   Handout #30, "Some Questions"

Procedure   1. Distribute a copy of Handout #30 to each student. Ask students to answer each of the items. Allow about ten minutes for this.

2. Ask how many persons think they got a perfect score. Explain to the group that they have just answered twenty-one selected items from the sixty-six item Alabama literacy test. Explain that you, as registrar, could deny any person in the room the right to vote, even if they missed only one of the items.

3. Spend a couple of minutes presenting the background to the literacy test as outlined in the introduction above.

SOME QUESTIONS

1. A United States senator at the general election in November takes office the following year on what date? _____

2. A person appointed to the United States Supreme Court is appointed for a term of _____.

3. When the Constitution was approved by the original colonies, how many states had to ratify it in order for it to be in effect? _____

4. Does enumeration affect the income tax levied on citizens in various states? _____

5. Persons opposed to swearing an oath may say, instead: "I solemnly _____."

6. What words are required by law to be on all coins and paper currency of the United States? _____

7. Appropriation of money for the armed services can be only for a period limited to _____ years.

8. The Constitution protects an individual against punishments which are _____ and _____.

9. Who passes laws dealing with piracy? _____

10. For security, each state has a right to form a _____.

11. Of the original 13 states, the one with the largest representation in the first congress was _____.

12. Capital punishment is the giving of a death sentence. (True or False)

13. "Involuntary servitude" is permitted in the United States upon conviction of a crime. (True or False)

14. If a state is a party to a case, the Constitution provides that original jurisdiction shall be in _____.

15. The Constitution limits the size of the District of Columbia to _____.

16. The only laws which can be passed to apply to an area in a federal arsenal are those passed by _____ provided consent for the purchase of the land is given by the _____.

17. Congress is composed of _____.

18. Money is coined by order of: _____ Congress _____ President _____ State.

19. If a person flees from justice into another state, who has authority to ask for his return? _____

20. If the two houses of Congress cannot agree on Adjournment, who sets the time? _____

21. After the presidential electors have voted, to whom do they send the count of their votes? _____

Introduction   One way of checking how images become part of the media in our society and the functional and dysfunctional aspect of media images is to watch TV. Several TV programs have ethnic and racial themes and in other shows, minorities play continuing roles. Students might consider watching some of these shows and reporting back to the class about how they believe ethnic groups are portrayed in the television media.

Objective   Students will be able to:

• Analyze a TV program and how ethnic and racial groups are portrayed.

Grade Level   7-12

Time   Two to three class periods

Materials   Current local TV guide
Handout #31, "Things to Look For"
Handout #32, "Portrayal of Minorities on TV Unreal"

Procedure   1. Divide the class into groups of three or four. Look at a local TV schedule and decide how you want to divide up the viewing and analyzing tasks. Each person is to watch at least one ethnic TV show, and fill out the worksheet after watching the show. Each person should then be prepared to report back to other members of the small groups in order to share and prepare for a class discussion.

In the United States and Canada, the following shows are shown. Adapt as needed for your students.

Fresh Prince of Belair	In Living Color	Martin
Old movies, especially	South Central	Living Singles
Cosby Show (reruns)	Commercials	the '30s, '40s and '50s

2. Each person in all groups should receive a copy of Handout #31

3. After all members of the small groups have viewed their assigned programs, filled in the handout, and reported back to members of their small groups, the groups should then prepare a groups report for the rest of the class.

Follow-up   1. Each group should use about ten minutes to report on the following: How Ethnic and Racial Groups Are Portrayed in the Television Media.

2. Have students read Handout #32 and then discuss whether the program they watched fit this picture.

TV GUIDE: THINGS TO LOOK FOR

Your name _____

TV program you watched _____

1. State briefly what the show was about.

2. Which ethnic group was portrayed in the show?

3. What specific things were said about the particular ethnic group?

4. In what positive ways do you think the ethnic/racial group(s) you watched were portrayed? What negative ways?

5. In your judgment, what was the point of including a show of this nature on TV?

6. Why do you think there is a demand for shows that deal with an ethnic group?

7. Why would people who are either a part or not a part of the ethnic group portrayed have an interest in viewing the show?

PORTRAYAL OF MINORITIES ON TV UNREAL

A core of overwhelmingly white producers and writers are "creating characters in their own image," producing artificial portrayals of blacks and other minorities on TV, a women's group has charged.

"Racial tension is commonplace in the real world, but virtually invisible among white and minority characters on entertainment television," concluded Sally Steenland, author of a Ford Foundation-financed study on how minorities are portrayed in the media.

The study Unequal Picture: Black, Hispanic, Asian and Native American Characters on Television was released by Wider Opportunities for Women, a non-profit group.

Among its major findings:

- Nine of 10 minority characters are middle class or wealthy where "in reality more than 40% of minority men and 60% of minority women have incomes below $10,000 a year."

- "Most programs reduce injustice to individual conflict, denying the reality of oppressive social structures, except for a very few shows which present a multicultureal world."

- Workplaces are portrayed as "egalitarian . . . with no hint of bias, even though whites are almost always in charge."

The study examined more than 150 episodes of 30 network television series featuring minorities in recurring roles.

Of the 78 minority characters on prime time TV, the study found that the overwhelming majority, 65--or 83%--were blacks. Blacks account for about 55% of the nation's minority population, according to Census Bureau data.

Hispanics accounted for only 12% of the minority characters on TV while they compose about 35% of the minority population. Asians, about 6% of the minority population, constituted about 4% of the minority characters on TV.

Indians constituted only 1% of the minority characters portrayed on TV. In reality, Native Americans make up about 2% of the minority population.

Reprinted by permission of Associated Press, August 1989.

©CTIR
University of Denver

Introduction
The quoted material on the handout accompanying this activity describes various types of racism. As a part of cultural awareness, students should develop cognitive tools for recognizing and dealing with racism, particularly its institutional forms. This activity offers some guidelines as possible tools.

Objectives
Students will be able to:

- Define racism.
- Distinguish between individual and institutional forms of racism.

Grade Level
10-12

Time
One class period

Materials
Handout #33, "Racism: Institutional Dimensions"

Procedure
1. Distribute a copy of the handout to each student. Ask students to look over the case examples and be ready to discuss them.

2. In the class discussion, ask:

- From the handout, how would you distinguish individual racism from institutional racism? (Students could mention that institutional forms involve both overt and covert discimination, involve policies, and are largely sanctioned by the institutions themselves.)

- In the examples given, which represent racist behavior and which do not? How did you make your determination? Which examples involve individual racism? Which institutional? How did you make your determination?

119

©CTIR
University of Denver

RACISM: INSTITUTIONAL DIMENSIONS

On Racism

In considering the diagnostic value of the concept of racism, we need to start with a definition. The word is a relatively new one and it is employed in different senses. One of the first writers to make extended use of it was Ruth Benedict in a book that in its London edition was given the title RACE AND RACISM (1940). She comes nearest to a definition when she writes that "racism is the dogma that one ethnic group is condemned by nature to congenital inferiority and another group is destined to congenital superiority." Social scientists have, in general, followed this lead in viewing racism as essentially a doctrine. The kernel of this doctrine is found in the assertions: (a) that people's culture and psychological characteristics are genetically determined; and (b) that the genetic determinants are grouped in patterns that can be identified with human races in the old morphological sense that envisaged the existence of pure races. Grouping these features, I have defined racism as the doctrine that a man's behavior is determined by stable inherited characteristics deriving from separate racial stocks having distinctive attributes and usually considered to stand to one another in relations of superiority and inferiority . . . .

However we define racism we have to contend with its pejorative connotation. It is not a neutral word. It has been said that in the social sciences our concepts tend to become epithets, but Everett Hughes remarks that in sociology many of our concepts were epithets before we took them up. He writes, "a considerable part of sociology consists of cleaning up the language in which common people talk of social and moral problems. We make great efforts to make bad things better by change of name, and we try, too, to make things disappear by giving them bad names. This used to be called "exorcism'" (1952:131). Racism is at present both a concept and an epithet. We cannot prevent its being an epithet but if, as sociologists, we wish to use it for diagnostic purposes, then we should try to use it in a systematic manner. I shall contend that our desire to use it as an epithet has muddied its use as a concept and may therefore have supported an error in diagnosis that hampers the campaign against intolerance . . . .

(Michael Banton, "The Concept of Racism")

On Institutional Racism

Negroes in America have been subject to "victimization" in the sense that a system of social relations operates in such a way as to deprive them of a chance to share in the more desirable materials and nonmaterial products of a society which is dependent, in part, upon their labor and loyalty. They are "victimized," also, because they do not have the same degree of access which others have to the attributes needed for rising in the general class system--money, education, contacts, and know-how.

(St. Claire Drake)

Racism is both overt and covert. It takes two, closely related forms: individual whites acting against individual Blacks, and acts by the total white community against the Black community. We call these individual racism and institutional racism. The first consists of overt acts by individuals, which cause death, injury, or the violent destruction of property. This type can be reached by television cameras; it can frequently be observed in the process of commission. The second type is less overt, far more subtle, less identifiable in terms of specific individuals committing the acts. But it is no less destructive of human life. The second type originates in the operation of established and respected forces in the society, and thus receives far less public condemnation than the first type.

(Stokely Carmichael and Charles V. Hamilton)

What white Americans have never fully understood--but what the Negro can never forget-- is that white society is deeply implicated in the ghetto. White institutions created it, white institutions maintain it, and white society condones it.

(Report of the National Advisory Commission of Civil Disorders)

Any institutional activity which creates racial inequalities, and results in the subordination and oppression of minorities, whether it be intentional or the result of "business as usual," is institutional racism. Blatant acts of institutional racism, such as separate educational, social, and recreational facilities, poll taxes, and literacy tests, have been largely eliminated as a result of litigations and legislation. It is the subtle acts remaining that are so debilitating. This form of racism is apparent in all the major institutions--educational, political, religious, economic, legal, health and welfare, and communications. These institutions are created by individuals for their benefit, and they operate under the auspices of customs, laws, mores, habits, and other cultural sanctions. Therefore, institutional racism is an extension of individual racism and indicative of the racism inherent in the culture.

Institutional racism appears in many forms. Colleges and universities, which proclaim to treat all applicants for admission equally, irrespective of ethnic identity, and judge them on the merits of their qualifications yet continue to use standardized tests as the evaluative criteria, are committing institutional racism. The judicial system, which grants a personal bond of $1,0000 to a white confessed and thrice-convicted felon accused of murder, but denies bail to a Black man accused of selling a marihuana cigarette to an undercover agent, and allows a Mexican American who has been declared mentally incompetent to be tried and convicted of first degree murder, is guilty of practicing racism. So is the economic system which lays claim to "free enterprise," but disqualifies ethnic minorities because of their racial and ethnic identity, and exploits them as consumers; the communications system which habitually paints negative stereotypic views of Blacks, Chicanos, and Puerto Ricans in newspaper reporting and advertising; the political system which spends billions of dollars annually to put a man on the moon, but allows poverty and starvation to continue to exist in this land of plenty. Thus, institutional racism is a "fact of American life," whether committed by design or effect, by intent or ignorance, by bigotry or naiveté. In its subtle form it is extremely difficult to detect and to determine who is at fault.

(Geneva Gay, "Racism in America:
Imperatives for Teaching Ethnic Studies")

Case Examples

Example One

A large university requires all its prospective enrollees to take the same entrance exam, which is written in English and based solely on the students' knowledge of classical European literature and history.

Example Two

As a result of a survey a local school board decides against instituting a bilingual/bicultural, English/Spanish curriculum. The school is comprised of over twenty-five ethnic groups other than Hispanic and Anglo. The board feels it would be impossible to implement the bilingual/bicultural program without being unfair to all the other ethnic groups in the school.

Example Three

In one neighborhood during the past two years a grocery store has prosecuted over 200 cases involving shoplifting. In 93 percent of the cases, those prosecuted were black Americans. As a result, the store manager has decided to put up a sign which states, "All black customers are subject to search before leaving the store."

Example Four

In an "honors" program of a university, Anglo students were given a letter stating they must maintain a 3.0 grade point average in order to stay in the program. Minority students were sent a letter stating they had to maintain no more than a 2.0 grade point average to stay in the "honors" program.

Introduction

In this activity, students identify and think about the geographic location of ethnic groups within a community. The ideas as reflected in the maps are then compared with the actual ethnic distribution as found within the students' community.

Objective

Students will be able to:

• Recognize feelings and thoughts about the population distribution in the "ideal" multicultureal community.

Grade Level

5-12

Time

One class period

Materials

Handout #34, "Plan A Community"
Handout #35, "Sample Maps"

Procedure

1. Distribute Handout #34 to students and ask them to fill it in the way they believe the IDEAL community should be organized.

2. Distribute Handout #35 which indicates four ways to distribute the groups. Ask students to study the samples. Draw them on the chalkboard. Have students compare their maps with those on the chalkboard.

3. Ask students:

• Why did you distribute the groups the way you did?

• What kinds of problems would be <u>solved</u> by your scheme?

• What kinds of problems might be <u>created</u> by your scheme?

• What problems do you think would be solved/created by your map?

• What can happen if <u>differences</u> are emphasized in a community?

• What can happen if <u>similarities</u> are emphasized in a community?

4. Obtain a street map of your community and see if students can identify and draw boundaries that identify cultural or ethnic neighborhoods. Ask:

_____

This activity was adapted from materials developed by Jarrell McCracken, Manual High School, Denver Public Schools, Denver, Colorado.

©CTIR
University of Denver

- Does this map resemble the one you drew or one drawn by the teacher? Describe.

5. Identify some of the factors that interacted to account for the location of people in your community. Write down two actions that, if taken, would result in your community's ethnic boundaries resembling those on the "ideal" map you drew.

Follow-up

1. Add other groups to the map such as income groups and special populations that are often isolated--senior citizens and physically challenged youth and adults.

2. Have students interview two or three people. Students should ask them to give five reasons why people live in culturally separated neighborhoods. Which of these reasons makes sense to you? Which don't?

PLAN A COMMUNITY

Distribute the ethnic population showing the geographic location where you think these groups should live.

KEY: Each:
M	represents	Chicanos	(MMMMMMMMM)
C	"	Chinese	(CCCCC)
E	"	English	(EEEEEEEEEEEEEEEEEEE)
B	"	Blacks	(BBBBBBBBB)
G	"	Germans	(GGGGGGGGG)
+	"	Cubans	(+++)
V	"	Vietnamese	(VV)
I	"	Irish	(IIIIIIIII)
O	"	Italians	(OOOOO)
P	"	Polish	(PPPPP)

©CTIR
University of Denver

SAMPLE MAPS

1. **Total Assimilation**

2. **Total Separation**

3. **Partial Assimilation**

4. **Complete Separation of Two Groups, Remainder Assimilated**

127

Introduction

Having students evaluate the school's handling of cultural studies and ethnic differences can be an important way for them to study discrimination in an institutional setting. Below are some guidelines in the form of a questionnaire should you and your students decide to make a evaluation of your school.

Objectives

Students will be able to:

• Analyze attitudes in the school towards cultural issues.
• Evaluate the adequacy of school policy and programs in meeting the needs of students' heritage's.

Grade Level

5-12

Time

One class period

Material

Handout #36, "Culture and Our School." Photocopy enough to survey 10 percent of the student body, faculty, and staff of the school, plus five extra copies.

Procedure

1. Divide class into groups of five or six to conduct the survey. Give each group enough copies of Handout #36 to conduct a part of the survey. The survey should be administered randomly; that is, students should select respondents on a nondiscriminatory basis.

2. Have one of the groups compile a master list of responses using a blank copy of the handout as the others bring in the completed forms.

3. Run off a transparency of the results, or record them on the chalkboard.

4. Hold a class discussion on how different cultures are treated in the school and discuss each item.

Follow-up

1. Devise a program to emphasize cultural ethnic and multiethnic heritage in the school.

2. Have students write an article for the school newspaper to praise the school's strong points.

3. Adapt the survey to address cultural issues such as the treatment of men and women in the school.

4. Write suggestions to improve the school in those areas where it is weakest. Present or give these ideas to someone who can help implement such improvements.

CULTURE AND OUR SCHOOL

You have been selected to participate in a school survey conducted by _____
_____ class in _____
Below is a list of statements. You are asked to place a check mark (√) in one of the three columns by each of the statements. You do not have to anwer all of the questions. Your participation is voluntary. Should you decide to include other comments, please do so on the back of the survey. Thank you for your time.

RATING			GUIDELINES
Strongly	Somewhat	Hardly at all	
			1. Are cultural differences apparent in your school?
			2. Are cultural differences emphasized in the school curriculum (courses, textbooks, other materials, teachers' and students' attitudes, etc.)?
			3. Does your school library and resource center have a variety of materials of the histories, experiences, and cultures of many different groups (including young and old, men and women)?
			4. Do school assemblies, speakers, holidays, etc., reflect cultural differences?
			5. Do extra-curricular activities include most groups present in your school?
			6. Do school policies make provisions for recognizing and commemorating the holidays and festivities of different ethnic groups?

	RATING		GUIDELINES
Strongly	Somewhat	Hardly at all	
			7. Do school policies respect the dignity and worth of students as individuals _and_ as members of special groups?
			8. Does the makeup (numbers) of the school staff reflect the ethnic and cultural makeup of the community?
			9. Do the courses reflect the diverse learning styles of students within the school community?
			10. Do you feel that teaching in the school is designed to help students live better in a multiethnic, multicultureal society?

©CTIR
University of Denver